COUNTRY LIVING
collection style

COUNTRY LIVING
collection

style

arranging and displaying your treasures

MARIE PROELLER HUESTON

HEARST BOOKS

A Division of Sterling
Publishing Co., Inc.
New York

Library of Congress Cataloging-in-Publication Data
Available upon request.

10 9 8 7 6 5 4 3

Book design by Patricia Fabricant

First Paperback Edition 2006
Published by Hearst Books
A Division of Sterling Publishing Co., Inc.
387 Park Avenue South, New York, NY 10016

Country Living and Hearst Books are registered trademarks of Hearst Communications, Inc.

www.countryliving.com

For information about custom editions, special sales, premium and corporate purchases, please contact Sterling Special Sales Department at 800-805-5489 or specialsales@sterlingpub.com.

Distributed in Canada by Sterling Publishing
c/o Canadian Manda Group, 165 Dufferin Street
Toronto, Ontario, Canada M6K 3H6

Distributed in Australia by Capricorn Link (Australia) Pty. Ltd.
P.O. Box 704, Windsor, NSW 2756 Australia

Manufactured in China

Sterling ISBN-13: 978-1-58816-566-4
        ISBN-10: 1-58816-566-3

CASE PHOTOGRAPHS: *front*, Charles Maraia; *back*, Steven Randazzo; *spine*, Michael Luppino.

PAGE ONE: A recent trend in home design finds collectors removing antique dinnerware from its traditional dining-room setting and placing it in living rooms, foyers, bedrooms, and many other settings throughout the house. When displayed in these unexpected spots, the objects become important decorative elements in the room. Brown-and-white transferware graces this living-room mantel. The largest pieces in the collection (the platter and the pitcher) have been set at the center and the outer edge of the mantel. Care was taken to alternate dense and airy border patterns to create a balanced look among the platter and plates. The addition of fresh fruit and flowers enlivens any arrangement.

PAGES 2 AND 3: A still life of flowers, art pottery, and a painting is artfully arranged on this ledge. (See also page 66.)

contents

WE HAVE A SAYING AT *COUNTRY LIVING* that three of anything makes a collection. If that's truly the case, then I own quite a few collections! Each type of object I'm drawn to has a distinct personality, whether it's the graceful curves of white McCoy pottery, the subtle nuances of black-and-white photography, or the glitzy glamour of beaded fruit. Different as they may be, these groupings all evoke the same emotion when I look at them—pure joy.

For me, spotting things I love has never been a challenge. (There's nothing I enjoy more than spending a weekend morning scouring the aisles of a flea market or exploring the nooks and niches of an antique shop.) The challenge has always been deciding how to display my finds in new and creative ways once I get them home. Let's face it, there are only so many options one has when lining a shelf with lovely things. Do you know where I turn when I've run out of ideas? The pages of *Country Living.*

Month after month we feature homes where imaginative owners showcase their collections in an interesting manner. Objects traditionally stored in cupboards are often hung on the walls, items intended for the walls might parade along a mantel, and classic mantel-top elements like urns and candlesticks frequently show up in bedrooms, kitchens, and other unexpected places. *Country Living Collection Style* is a compilation of my favorite ideas from recent years. Let it inspire you to bring your beloved collections to the forefront in your home, where they can evoke in you the same joyous feeling my collections evoke in me.

—Nancy Mernit Soriano
Editor in Chief, *Country Living*

Collections need not be large to make a grand statement in the home. Consider this simple grouping of milk glass: Not only does the arrangement create visual interest in a room, it also hints at the many variations of pattern, form, and color that exist within this area of collecting. Windowsills are ideal spots to display transparent or translucent objects; sunlight makes them glow. Illumination in the evening can be achieved with votive candles placed nearby.

introduction

Part of the joy of owning antiques and heirlooms is being able to use them in everyday life. Highlights from an art pottery collection form a festive centerpiece on this dining-room table. Although each of the four vases has a distinct design, the choice to place one large and one small example on either side of the fruit bowl creates a sense of symmetry. A thoughtful layering of linens—an embroidered tea towel atop a linen tablecloth—sets the stage for the arrangement.

PICTURE IF YOU WILL A SINGLE SCULPTURAL OBJECT set on a gleaming tabletop. Beautiful and elegant, to be sure, but a bit solitary as well. Now add a second, similar item to the scene. Suddenly the two pieces begin to complement one another, inviting comparison and closer inspection. Add a third and the visual impact only increases. In a nutshell, this scenario illustrates the inspiration behind building a collection. If you found your own interest piqued as the number of objects increased, then you are a collector at heart. For you, there is power in numbers. For you, less is never more. And it is to you that this book is dedicated.

Whether intrigued by quilts or books or vintage toasters, all collectors share a passion for the basic process of gathering. They thrive on the thrill of the hunt, waking at dawn to be among the first entrants to a flea market or rummage sale. Their pulses quicken when a desirable piece comes into view amid a jumble of junk. They revel in haggling with dealers to get the lowest price. The best part? Proudly showing new purchases to friends, family, and fellow enthusiasts. But what is it that drives a person to accumulate multiple items in the first place? Certainly there is no need to own twenty ironstone pitchers, forty printed tablecloths, or one hundred Brownie cameras. Need, collectors are quick to point out, never enters into the equation. Rather, the key factor here is fun: Life is simply more enjoyable when searching for and surrounded by the things you love.

A favorite collection can sometimes inspire the decoration of an entire room. One particularly ardent Jade-ite enthusiast enlarged the Fire-King logo and made a stencil for his kitchen walls; a paint store was able to match the glassware's distinctive green hue. Below the stencils, a row of Jade-ite mugs hangs from tiny hooks. Framed Fire-King advertising graces the wall above the stencils.

The impulse to collect is by no means a modern phenomenon. For centuries, the upper classes around the world have filled rooms in their homes with fine paintings and porcelain, exotic plants, and other treasures that would immediately convey to visitors the wealth and good taste of their hosts. Antique portraits often depict successful merchants and landowners grouped with their possessions in an effort to preserve the collection (and the prestige of the sitter) for posterity. It wasn't until the nineteenth century that collecting became a pastime for the average citizen as well. Along with the technological advances it ushered in, the Industrial Revolution also brought with it the development of a middle class that had both leisure time and disposable income. This burgeoning group looked to the wealthy for ideas about cultured activities and sophisticated interior design—hence the widespread popularity of gathering and arranging precious objects in one's place of residence.

So prevalent was the tendency to collect and display during the last quarter of the 1800s, in fact, that no proper Victorian parlor would have been considered complete without abundant accessories scattered throughout the room, such as Currier & Ives prints on the walls, pressed flowers in rustic frames on the mantel, porcelain figurines on bookshelves, and shell-encrusted boxes on tabletops. This unbridled zeal for incorporating collections into interior design schemes continued well into the twentieth century, sparking a thriving market for home design magazines that carried new ideas for presentation to urban and rural subscribers alike—a market that has only grown stronger with each passing year.

Today the trend to display collections around the house endures, although it's no longer a matter of showing off one's wealth or imitating the upper class. American home owners surround themselves with treasured antiques and collectibles for one simple reason: to beautify and personalize their dwellings. Indeed, the range of objects that can be collected is as limitless as the imagination, and each person may truly blaze his own trail when it comes to decorating his home. Even when two people appreciate the same subject matter, no two collections—and no two displays—are ever exactly the same.

Another noticeable difference between collecting then and now is that currently, eclectic tastes and unique visions are embraced like never before. Years ago, the types of collections considered proper for indoor display encompassed fairly traditional themes—silver, pewter, glass, china, woven textiles, and the like. Today, anything goes. Not that traditional objects have gone out of style or ever will, but these days vintage lunch boxes, wooden potato mashers, colorful swizzle sticks, and well-worn sporting equipment are considered equally worthy of a place of honor, as

The strong graphics and faded colors of antique game boards make them a popular decorating device. Layering the smaller examples in front of the larger ones adds dimension to the small grouping without detracting from the painted patterns. (A similar layering approach also works well when arranging select groups of framed prints, photographs, or paintings.) Offsetting the wooden boards with a single ceramic piece with strong vertical ribbing enlivens the display.

are the finest vases or the most exquisite needlework.

Although all collectors share the compulsion to gather, the attraction to one particular item over another is intensely personal and can vary widely from one individual to the next. For some people, the connection to a certain type of object may stem from nostalgic feelings about an era or experience—a fond memory of a grandfather's pocket watch, for instance, or the collectibles associated with a favorite childhood television show. That's how it was for Jeff Snyder, a Minnesota collector whose 1920s home was featured in the July 2000 issue of *Country Living*. When he first began to enjoy antiquing, Snyder found himself buying the occasional Jade-ite plate or mug at flea markets and antiques stores because the sturdy green pieces

Nearly every item on display in this sitting room conveys the owners' passion for the sea—from the vintage beach pails on the coffee table to the anchor-motif shutters flanking the window. A dominant color scheme of red, white, and blue prevents the copious collection from overpowering the small space. Carefully placed details throughout the room (the bathing-beauty hatbox, the row of nautical flags, the pile of pillows on the sofa, the hooked rug above the window) encourage the eye to move from floor to ceiling and back again.

reminded him of his grandmother's kitchen. Fast forward two decades, and Snyder's collection of Jade-ite and other Fire-King glassware has ballooned to more than 5,000 examples, filling cupboards, bookshelves, and special display units in his house. He even stenciled the Fire-King logo onto his kitchen walls and hung the company's vintage advertising in frames around the room.

For other people, the urge to collect may originate with an inexplicable response to an aesthetic form. Such was the case for Electra Havemeyer Webb (1888–1960), legendary collector of American folk art and founder of Vermont's esteemed Shelburne Museum. As the daughter of one of the wealthiest businessmen in Victorian

America, Webb spent her childhood in elegant homes decorated with her parents' European master paintings and fine antiques. When she reached adulthood, her first impulse was to continue collecting the types of items she'd grown up with. Her true calling, however, would not emerge until one fateful day in rural New England. While driving through a picturesque Connecticut village, Webb spotted a cigar store Indian outside a tobacconist's shop. Something about the humble form spoke to her, and she quickly purchased it from the storekeeper for $15 and brought it home.

Thus began Webb's lifelong love affair with American folk art. It didn't take long for the objects she amassed—primitive portraits, hooked rugs, duck decoys, and patchwork quilts, to name a few—to fill the rooms in her house and a number of other structures on the property as well (guests playing tennis on the Webbs' indoor court, for example, had to be careful not to trip over "spectators"—or the figural sculptures lining the sides of the court). It's important to note that, unlike today, there was little appreciation for American folk art when Webb began col-

Concentrating a sizable collection in a limited amount of space heightens the visual impact of the pieces. Here, seashell crafts of all descriptions share two shelves with other ocean-related items such as a dried starfish, a cast-iron ship doorstop, and images of the shore. Though the overall look is energetic, objects are lined up in simple rows so that proper attention can be paid to each intricate creation. Varying the height of the objects underscores their range of designs. The central element on the top shelf is the lowest, while large and small items are alternated on the bottom shelf.

ABOVE: A small collection of carved wood, ceramic, and painted composition heads becomes the focal point of this light-filled living room when paired with eclectic objects on a warm wood table. Antique books and a time-worn trunk serve double duty in the display: They provide various heights on which to place each piece, while mirroring the aged surfaces of the heads. In a more modern interior, the collection might have been arranged in a simple row on a mantel or art shelf, resulting in a drastically different look.

lecting early in the 1900s. In fact, Webb's mother became so distraught over her daughter's choices that she was provoked to exclaim, "How can you, Electra, you who have been brought up with Rembrandts and Manets, live with such American trash?" Webb stood firm in the face of her mother's skepticism, however, and instead heeded the words of her father, H. O. Havemeyer: "It takes nerve as well as taste to be a collector."

That is sound advice for any collector. Still, once we've zeroed in on and accumulated the items we love, an important question remains unanswered: How do we arrange these possessions in our homes to best showcase the breadth and energy of the collection? That's where *Country Living Collection Style* comes in. For more than a quarter century, *Country Living* has visited homes filled with wonderful antiques and gleaned useful tips from collectors, dealers, decorators, architects, curators, and conservators. Country style and collection display have evolved a great deal since the magazine first appeared on newsstands in 1978, and our editors have tracked every trend along the way. Between the covers of this book, you'll find all the information we've learned over the years condensed into one indispensable volume.

We start at the beginning with The Art of Arranging. Because before you can turn your attention to the rooms in which your precious possessions will spend their days, you must analyze the items themselves. How should they be placed next to one another to best highlight each piece? Are the objects fragile and in need of an enclosed haven or are they solid and able to be positioned anywhere in the house? Will your collections look best in rows or clusters? Small or large groupings? These questions and others like them are the first things to consider when starting any interior design project.

Next, in a chapter entitled Decorating with Collections, we explore how to incorporate diverse objects into a setting and how that placement will affect and determine a room's overall appearance. In order to achieve the highest level of success, home owners must examine their own personal style. Do you prefer a pared

OPPOSITE: Collections do more than merely bring visual interest to an interior; they also personalize a home. This quirky roundup of Os succeeds on both counts. Not only does it solve the age-old problem of what to do with bare wall space, it also reveals its owner's fondness for her initial. When building a collection like this, think artistically. In addition to decorating with actual letters, this creative individual also selected similar shapes in transferware plates, a small wire basket, and a fanciful metal fragment.

down look or one that is joyfully over the top? Do your possessions date to a particular era that may offer inspiration regarding display—High Victorian, perhaps, or 1950s Modern—or are they an eclectic mix that will require a fresh approach? What are the particulars regarding the layout of each room? How can you find a room's focal point and what should you put there?

Additional concerns are addressed in the third chapter, Making Objects Look Their Best. Here you'll find out about choosing the best lighting to highlight your possessions, creating an ideal display space when one does not already exist in a room, deciding upon a regular schedule of care and cleaning, and much more. Finally, in Three of Anything Makes a Collection, we demonstrate how even the smallest collections (three in particular) can become a memorable presence in interior design. Throughout the book, Decorator's Tips provide tricks of the trade regarding such topics as how to make small groupings appear larger, how to turn postcards into fine art, and how best to store your cherished objects when they're not on display. Whatever your personal style or individual concerns may be, we hope the photographs and advice found in *Collection Style* will spark wonderful ideas for every room in your house.

OPPOSITE: A crystal chandelier adds a touch of glamour to this country dining room. The tall glass-fronted cabinet is an ideal repository for an ironstone collection. The owner paid careful attention to placement behind the doors: pitchers, platters, covered serving dishes, and other items are mixed together on the shelves (as opposed to all the plates and platters on one shelf, all the pitchers on another) to achieve a lively look. Three imposing pitchers and a covered serving piece act as a crown on top of the cabinet. Beautiful table linens are a simple way to add color—whether a soft hint or a bold punch—to a neutral space.

RIGHT: In a sunny kitchen, an assortment of silver candlesticks are grouped together on a marble countertop. The placement creates a feeling of depth while allowing each design to be viewed in full silhouette. Candles can be chosen to reflect a home's dominant color scheme; in this case, white and cream were combined. Amateur floral still lifes—like the dried hydrangea painting seen here—can also complement a room's decor.

one

The Art of Arranging

IN THE DRAWING ROOM OF HER POSH PARK AVENUE APARTMENT, twentieth-century cosmetics queen Helena Rubinstein (1871–1965) covered the walls with paintings by art world luminaries including Dalí, Degas, Matisse, Modigliani, Picasso, and Renoir. One critic scoffed at the collection, claiming that many of the images did not represent the best work of the artists. Rubinstein was unperturbed. "Quality's nice," she reportedly responded, "but quantity makes a show." She was right. For while quality is certainly not something a collector should overlook, it is *quantity*—or the grouping of multiple objects—that creates the strongest visual drama in an interior. More important, displaying similar items en masse allows a collection to transcend its physical attributes and clearly capture and convey the passions of its owners.

Creating arrangements that attain such lofty goals as transcending, capturing, and conveying (not to mention just looking good in a particular setting) is not always easy. More likely than not, we all know someone for whom this comes naturally: A person who is able to set three flowerpots on a windowsill or organize a half-dozen perfume bottles on a vanity and have the resulting vignette look as if it just popped out of a magazine. Most of us, however, require some assistance when it comes to winnowing the contents of our boxes, bags, cupboards, and closets into eye-catching displays. To succeed, we must begin by carefully analyzing what we own to determine what type of placement will best showcase the size and scope of the collection.

The first things to consider are the physical qualities of the objects in your collection. Are they three-dimensional or flat? Sturdy or fragile? Big or small? If the items are very large or heavy—garden statuary, for example, or stoneware jugs—your ability to display many at once may be compromised in most traditional settings. One solution would be to line them up along the floor in a part of the house with limited foot traffic. Another might involve arranging small clusters (three or four at a time work well together) throughout several rooms. At the other end of the size scale, diminutive collectibles—such as thimbles, buttons, or miniature chairs—present their own set of concerns. Because tiny things can get lost in expansive settings, they can benefit from placement within a specialized display space. Some possibilities include a shadow box, a coffee table topped with a glass display case, and a small platform or "stage" set on top of a larger tabletop. A stage can be anything from a thick slab of beveled glass to a decorative toleware tray on which a selection of tiny items like inkwells, bud vases, or animal figurines can be featured.

The next step in the process is to judge the numeric size of your collection in relation to the amount of display space that is available in your home. Owners of small collections (or collections in progress) may have only ten or twenty items that need to be arranged. For obvious reasons, these people will have more placement options than people who have a lifetime of accumulated objects to contend with. These collections fit nicely on a single tabletop or along the living-room mantel. Anyone wishing to make a limited number of items appear more substantial can try one of the following tricks. Concentrate most of the collection on one tabletop (eight to ten vases on the dining-room sideboard, for instance), then place single pieces elsewhere in the house (maybe one vase in a still life in the foyer and another beside the telephone in the living room). This way the eye is registering a bit of the

collection in each room, making it seem as if there are enough objects to fill the house. Another idea involves grouping all the vases (or figurines or candy dishes or duck decoys) on a table or mantel and leaning a beautiful mirror behind them, thus doubling the visual impact of the arrangement.

By contrast, owners of collections that number in the hundreds or even thousands won't need the aid of a mirror. More likely, these folks will need to decide whether they want to (or are able to) display everything at once. If you are just such a collector and can't imagine parting with even one cherished item, you might be able to fill a cupboard or even dedicate an entire room to display, building rows of shelves to accommodate each piece. Many zealous collectors approach this predicament by rotating displays into and out of storage. Rotating collections is beneficial on a number of levels. First, it allows for a large collection to be viewed in more intimate groupings. Second, it protects precious collectibles from year-round exposure to sunlight, indirect light, dust, and accidental breakage. And last, changing displays several times a year keeps interiors fresh and exciting—a special point of interest for anyone who enjoys seasonal decorating such as swathing upholstered furniture in white slipcovers in the summer and burgundy velvet in the winter.

Whether your collection is large, small, or a perfectly manageable size, it's always wise to think creatively about places to display the pieces and to be on the lookout for additional or unusually attractive options when shopping at antiques stores, flea markets, or garage sales. All of these venues harbor traditional bookcases, hanging shelves, and glass cases. (A vintage display case from an old general store or candy shop can look wonderful in the house when filled with artifacts.) Leave yourself open to suggestions from untraditional items that can be used for display. A painted bench can support a row of old watering cans or enamelware pitchers; a wooden ladder can become a rack for quilts, coverlets, or decorative dish towels; a dressmaker's mannequin with a warm patina can sport a collection of costume jewelry around its neck or alligator belts around its waist; a handful of weathered iron coat hooks can be mounted on the wall and used for hanging straw boaters in a hallway; even a single side chair can become an artful easel for a lone painting or framed print. The possibilities are as endless as your imagination.

With the practical questions aside, collectors can now consider how they would like to group their possessions. By finding the common thread among disparate objects and highlighting those similarities, one can create beautiful arrangements in any room. If all the contents of a collection are essentially the same with only slight variations, a home owner's choices will be somewhat limited when it comes to combining objects, because the common thread between the items has already been determined. People who own multiple collections or a smattering of vintage odds and ends have more freedom with placement. Objects can be grouped by size (a combination of butter plates and salt cellars, perhaps); by shape (all circles or all cubes); or by theme (anything related to natural history, from fossils to flower

OPPOSITE AND ABOVE: In an unexpected twist on the traditional dining-room hutch, books are arranged inside the doors while silver and flatware remain outside. A collection of sterling and silverplate is split into two groups. Tall trophies and coffeepots (left unpolished to turn a dark patina) are kept on top; the ornate candlesticks are placed up front to ensure easy access at mealtime. On the lower surface, silver flatware is organized in both squat trophies, polished to match their contents, and a cut-glass condiment dish. The owner chose this type of display because she could not bear storing her beloved flatware collection out of sight in a drawer.

decorator's tip

Staggering the height of objects on display is one of the best ways to create visual drama in a room. In order to do this, it may be necessary to place some items on a pedestal. Many things can be called on to act as a pedestal—a cake stand, for instance, or an attractive wooden box. Stacks of books (like the ones used in this arrangement of mercury glass) are especially well suited to the task, because you can customize the height by altering the number of volumes used.

presses). It can be fun for decorators and guests alike to see the connections that link vastly different types of things. Imagine a collector with a penchant for pansies who spots the motif on an amateur Victorian still life, a 1940s printed tablecloth, 1950s juice glasses, paper candy boxes from the early 1900s, and ceramics from occupied Japan—what a lively display those items would make!

Grouping by color is another option open to anyone decorating with collections—and one that can result in particularly striking vignettes. It's possible that an entire collection would be of a single color, as would be the case with green Depression glass, white ironstone china, or bold red cast-iron toy fire trucks. Occupying the open shelves of a stately hutch or a glass-fronted corner cabinet fitted with internal lights, any one of those collections would look stunning. Another collector attracted to a single color might

Small arrangements highlight the sculptural qualities of collections. Here, a half dozen vases chosen for their graceful silhouettes are staggered on a tabletop. At least six inches of space is left between each example to make design variations easy to see. A green-plaid tablecloth echoes the color scheme underneath. Polished stone eggs are grouped in an alabaster fruit bowl; tactile collections like this one are best positioned where guests can see and touch individual pieces.

OPPOSITE: When properly displayed, ordinary objects can become the darlings of decorators. In this living room, for instance, a row of forced bulbs in terra-cotta flowerpots adorns the mantel. Ironstone platters—originally an inexpensive line of dinnerware when first introduced in the 1800s—now command attention on display in matching bookcases. To break up the large blocks of white, a shelf of books separates each platter. A single pitcher occupies each of the bottom shelves. Because the owner had only three large platters to work with, a trio of smaller designs takes the place of a fourth. A sculptural footstool and an elegant child's chair placed on top of the bookshelves draw the eye upwards.

ABOVE: To make a strong statement in a room, collections don't need to be extensive or made up of elegant silver or porcelain. Just look at these polished-stone balls: set on a mantel in a simple row, the quartet adds an artistic note to the setting. The home owners highlighted the subtle color variations in the stone by alternating light, medium, and dark tones in the arrangement.

choose to gather objects representing a variety of materials. This collector's hutch or corner cupboard might instead be brimming with a few pieces of green Depression glass, a selection of green McCoy planters, a dozen green Bakelite napkin rings, and several small stacks of vintage gardening books carefully positioned so that their moss-green spines and gold-embossed titles face outwards. Either approach is acceptable and makes for a display that is easy for viewers to admire.

When it comes to the exact placement of objects within a display, the aim should be for each item to be clearly seen, and for the overall effect to be one that looks intentional, not like a mass of things casually grouped together. Proper spacing will ensure a harmonious arrangement. The precise distance between pieces will depend in part on their size. You will be able to set smaller objects closer together than you would larger ones. To illustrate this point, imagine a cluster of salt-and-pepper shakers (which may require only an inch or less between each example to make each design discernable to the viewer's eye), compared with a row of stoneware crocks, which would surely look overcrowded with only an inch between each one. At least two to three inches separation is necessary for large crocks or other sizable pieces.

Varying the height within a display is also important, as this will add visual interest to the scene. In general, keep the tallest pieces towards the back of a group-

THE ART OF ARRANGING

ABOVE: Two small rows of antique containers are at once useful and pleasing to the eye. The owners use the decorative pieces to store cotton balls, lip balm, earrings, and other accessories. The gradation from small jars in the front to larger in the back was a natural choice for this group of objects. Set behind the jars in an ornate bowl, a selection of soaps resembles a display of precious objects.

RIGHT: Grid patterns and symmetrical arrangements are perfect for keeping sizable collections under control. In this bath, celluloid cold cream jars and cotton ball dispensers from the 1920s are lined up in neat rows on a small table.

ing on a tabletop, shelf, or mantel and then adjust the placement of short and medium objects in the foreground until a pleasing plan is achieved. If a collection is made up of items that are all the same size (such as six-inch cordial glasses or foot-tall cookie jars), you can vary the height within the arrangement by placing some items on top of other things. A short stack of books, a cake stand, or a beautiful wooden box would all work well as sturdy supports on which additional items can stand. Positioning one or more framed works of art behind an arrangement—a painting, print, or photograph, for example—is another way to add height.

There are times when rows will present a better display option than clusters. One situation where this would be the case is if all the items in a collection are the same height but possess design variations to which the owner wants to draw special attention (as could be the case with either enamelware coffeepots bearing different vibrant colors and graphic patterns, or the stoneware crocks described earlier). In a row, the coffeepots and crocks would be viewed as a collection but also as separate entities deserving closer inspection. Graduated sets of objects also look best when lined up in rows. Some examples are decorative tin canisters arranged on a kitchen countertop, or a collection of transferware pitchers parading along cupboard shelves in sizes ranging from a four-inch creamer to an eighteen-inch ewer.

This tabletop arrangement highlights one person's passion for plaid. Boxes, letter openers, napkin rings, and an hourglass are just a few of the objects on display. A wooden document box was placed on the table to provide an additional surface for display. Grouping similar items on different levels highlights them and calls attention to variations in individual pieces.

OPPOSITE: This sizable selection of all-white wares includes figurines, flower vases, urns, and more. Creating an arrangement that starts with the shortest item (an ivory-handled magnifying glass), and that gradually increases in height, allows each element to be seen. Using color as a unifying factor in a collection can create enjoyment for both home owner and guests. For the collector, it becomes a challenge to find as many variations on a theme as possible. For visitors, there is great appreciation and interest in what has been found.

Using what we've learned so far, let's look at three different collections and analyze how one might choose to display them in the home. The first collection is vintage kitchenware, gathered over a lifetime. It numbers in the hundreds and includes tin canisters and flour sifters, egg cups, novelty pot holders, copper molds, fruit and vegetable motif juice glasses, wood-handled potato mashers and egg beaters, Bakelite utensils, and Pyrex mixing bowls and refrigerator-ware. To begin with, let's examine the physical qualities of the collection: They are varied, and no category of objects is particularly delicate, so the display options open to the owner are almost limitless. The egg cups are small, however, and in danger of becoming lost among all the other items, so special attention should be focused on them. And, because the majority of detail on the copper molds is located on the tops of the pieces, hanging them on the wall probably makes the most sense.

Regarding placement, large collections like this one do well when separated into smaller, more manageable clusters. Grouping by theme would be natural for the copper molds, pot holders, and egg cups. The copper molds would appear dramatic on the wall above a dining-room sideboard; a series of especially whimsical pot holders could be framed and hung on the wall in the kitchen; the egg cups could be concentrated in a whitewashed wire spice rack unearthed at a flea market. This collection also makes possible a lively grouping by color, since it features so many pieces in so many hues. For instance, if the owner's kitchen were decorated in red and white (picture white walls, red-and-white gingham curtains, and red vinyl seats on retro-style

ABOVE: Finding a common thread among disparate objects can create some of the most evocative displays. Weathered surfaces and soft shades of blue and green link the items grouped on this table. With the exception of the architectural details behind the enamelware coffeepot, no two objects are alike. Lined up in a row, the three blue pieces form the foundation of the arrangement; the green and white elements were moved around until the most suitable spot was discovered.

kitchen chairs), a glass-front cupboard could be filled with red Pyrex, tomato-motif juice glasses, red-striped flour sifters, and red Bakelite-handled forks, knives, and spoons standing handle upwards in small white syrup pitchers. Beneath the cupboard, a prize set of graduated enamelware canisters featuring a lively red-and-white checked pattern would add the perfect finishing touch.

Let's see how display options change if the collection in question is one dozen antique quilts instead of hundreds of vintage kitchen items. The contents of this collection are unusual in that they can be both flat and, if folded or rolled, three-dimensional, creating numerous options for display. If most of the quilts were twin-size or larger, there would be more display options if they were folded, stacked, or draped than if they were opened out. Any quilts that were child, crib, or doll-size could be easily accommodated in any room. If ceiling height allows, quilt enthusiasts commonly choose to hang at least one quilt over a sofa or on an open wall in the house. When planning to hang large quilts, it's wise to prepare more than one design and to rotate the textiles once or twice a year, because antique fabrics and stitching can suffer under the weight and strain of hanging. Quilts that aren't currently on view need not be stored away; instead, they could await their turn on the wall while draped over a quilt rack or stacked in an old cupboard (every time the door was opened, their cheerful patterns could be seen and enjoyed).

When hung in the foyer, straw boaters call to mind lazy summer afternoons. Clustering them together on a wooden hat rack also draws attention to the many ribbon variations found here. Pinstriped wallpaper was chosen to mimic the seersucker suits men traditionally wore with this style of hat. There are many ways to use hats as decorative elements in the home. A selection of blue or yellow tulle designs (or any hue you like), for instance, infuses a room with color, while examples with ostrich feathers or wax flowers add a feminine touch to a bedroom, powder room, or dressing area. Particularly flamboyant designs are fun in little girls' rooms and can be taken down for dress-up time.

Depending on the particular patterns in the collection, antique quilts can be grouped by color (indigo and white, for instance, or red and green); by pattern (Log Cabin, Nine Patch, Double Wedding Ring); or by size (doll- or crib-size quilts). A blue bedroom could benefit from a quilt rack or wooden ladder over which a selection of indigo-and-white quilts was laid. A trio of doll quilts framed and hung in a row could enhance the décor of a nursery or playroom. And in a living room or den, a quilt display over the sofa could change with the seasons—charming red and green around the holidays, colorful flower baskets in the spring, and patriotic colors in the summer. When spotted in the marketplace, extremely time-worn quilts should not be passed over by textile enthusiasts: They can be salvaged and used as upholstery fabric for ottomans, wing chairs, and other accessories in the quilt lover's home.

Finally, let us consider a third collection: Flexible Flyer sleds and related memorabilia, such as framed vintage advertising and Lionel train-set figurines of little boys on sleds. The physical qualities of the diverse categories within this collection range from large and cumbersome (the sleds) and completely flat (the frames), to diminutive and dainty (the

When it comes to displaying antique quilts, draping a design over the top of a bed is just one of the many options open to collectors. Two other ideas can be seen in this loft-like living room, where a graphic pieced pattern hangs from the loft railing up above and additional examples are folded over the back and arm of the sofas. Positioning pillows in front of the sofa displays protects the quilts from the wear and tear they would receive if people were to leaned against them on a regular basis. Other collections help the room attain the perfect balance between country and contemporary looks. The overall look is airy and modern, but the quilts, the tower of picnic baskets, the doll's furniture on the coffee table, and the ironstone along the mantel add a decidedly old-fashioned touch. Positioning a single element in the kitchen (the doll's chair on the countertop) connects the two spaces.

ABOVE: Even the tiniest handful of pretty things, when properly situated, can enhance a room. Here, a watery blue bowl holds gifts from the sea. Encountering a bowl like this in an unexpected spot will make visitors to your home respond with delight. Marbles, foreign coins, dried seedpods, and other small items can be used as well. Treat the bowl's color as a background for the collection: Dark objects look best in a white or lightly shaded setting; clear or white items stand out against medium or dark hues.

OPPOSITE: Diminutive items that seem to beckon people to pick them up and have a closer look do well when presented at arm's reach. These early-1900s portrait pins are a perfect example. Arranging the portraits in a haphazard manner gives a more casual feeling than would lining them up in rows. Be sure that objects set out in such a way are pieces you don't mind guests handling. Exceptionally rare or fragile items might do better being placed inside a glass case before setting them out on a tabletop.

figurines). Therefore, each one requires a different approach when it comes to display. Depending on available wall space, either the sleds can be clustered together on one wall, or they can be spaced throughout the house (one over a sofa, headboard, or mantel, for instance, or two in the foyer flanking the front door). The framed ads might be lined up along the mantel or hung on the wall. (For specific tips on arranging frames on a wall, see "Arranging Frames," on page 132.) A pair of curvaceous side chairs on either side of a fireplace or dresser could each act as an easel for a framed ad. Because the figurines are so small, they can be placed anywhere. Still, they should be grouped together to make more of a statement. They might look fun sledding along a mantel, sharing space on a bookshelf with books and other collections, or—if there are enough of them—filling a special glass display case all by themselves.

If the ideal arrangement for your own collections is not immediately apparent, don't panic: Decorators often play with possessions for hours—deciding on mantel or cupboard, varying height and spacing, switching from row to cluster and back again—until one placement seems just right. By following these tips and trusting your instincts, your eye will eventually tell you when you've got it right.

BELOW: Matching frames is the easiest way to unify a collection of vintage prints. Elegant gold designs were chosen for these tree prints; the gilded frames add a sophisticated touch to the otherwise casual atmosphere of this seaside dining area. Prints are wonderful collections for decorating: botanical motifs can be paired with floral fabrics or used to accent an all-white room. Natural history designs such as snakes and frogs are great for little boys' rooms. Frames, too, can be found in colors and materials that enhance their surroundings—from sleek silver and dramatic black to feminine pastels and warm wood tones.

RIGHT: Framed collections can be hung on a wall, leaned up against a wall, or—as seen in this photograph—displayed both ways at once. In this case, the choice to do both creates a clear distinction between two different collections. Silhouettes are propped up against the wall beneath intricate cut-paper images. Positioning the small brown frame at the center of the arrangement creates a focal point. The added touch of fresh flowers in color-coordinated vases (a small black urn and a black-and-white sugar bowl missing its lid) softens the sharp angles of the black frames and cut paper.

decorator's tip

People are so accustomed to paying attention to what's inside a frame that they tend to overlook the frame itself. Not so for savvy decorators who recognize that these items are not only functional but frequently quite decorative. Adorning a wall with empty frames—whether in a row, in a grid pattern, or as a single aesthetic touch—adds interest to a room. Frame styles range from ornate gilded Victorian frames to rustic bent-twig Adirondack designs. Pairing empty frames with framed art is another attractive option.

OPPOSITE: This kitchen hutch illustrates one good way to display a collection of similar, yet not identical, objects. The majority of enamelware coffeepots and teapots are blue and white, tall and thin. For this reason, the most dissimilar among them (large, squat, and green and white) are placed in the center of the hutch, with the others framing it. Alternating blue and white designs creates a balanced look, while facing all the pots in the same direction unifies the group. Artful arrangements in the sunny breakfast nook include the plates on the wall (two large examples divided by a small row of three) and the centerpiece made up of painted flowerpots.

RIGHT: An avid gardener's breakfast area is filled with inspired ideas. Positioning plates on the wall adds a touch of grass-green to the neutral space; the more saturated shades are broken up with green-on-white designs and a trellis-style plant stand. Salvaged materials also evoke the great outdoors. A portion of whitewashed fencing hangs against the beaded-board paneling, while a weathered shutter acts as a swinging door between the kitchen and dining room. Cabbage-leaf bowls are ideal for this table setting.

LEFT: Each shelf of this country cupboard has been painstakingly arranged with ironstone so that the dinnerware is both attractive and accessible for everyday use. On the top shelf, three covered serving dishes stand in front of two dinner plates. Another option would have been to place a plate behind each of the serving dishes, but this uneven approach creates a more energetic feeling. A more symmetrical placement is found one shelf down, where each cup and saucer stands in front of a plate. (Cup handles are turned inward for a cleaner line.) Another shelf down finds four plates paired with a sugar bowl in the center, a gravy boat to the right, and small plates for butter pats throughout. On the bottom surface, mismatched bread and salad plates are stacked and interspersed with a set of four teacups, and antique linen napkins. Sturdy mugs are not only part of the overall display, they also act as useful storage for flatware.

OPPOSITE: For collectors who can't bear the thought of not displaying their collections, open shelves are a better option than cabinets in the kitchen. The owner of this sunny space felt that accessibility was just as important as visibility, so everything (with the exception of the row of ironstone pitchers and assorted items above the windows) is easy to reach. A set of brown-and-white ironstone dinnerware occupies two shelves between the sink and the stove; the twelve teacups hang from small hooks, clearing shelf space for plates, saucers, and serving pieces. More white ware fits neatly under the work island while vintage white-enameled colanders hang beneath an old coat rack under the blackboard.

THE ART OF ARRANGING

BELOW: A clear glass jar is a great receptacle for strawberry pincushions from the late 1800s and the ever popular tomato variety of the 1940s. Concentrating a large collection in a single spot works well, especially with tiny items, which tend to get lost when they are spread out in larger settings. The choice of container enhances the visual interest of the display: Not only will guests be intrigued by what's inside a lovely vintage jar like this one, they'll also appreciate your creativity in finding a new use for it.

ABOVE: Displaying objects in a setting other than the one for which they were originally intended makes viewers look twice. Taken off the tree and piled in a milk-glass compote, these Christmas ornaments create a fresh look on a windowsill. One major plus when displaying glass ornaments in this manner is that each one need not be perfect; you can use pristine examples or imperfect designs you find at flea markets for a few dollars apiece, or you can mix the two together. Without the greenery underneath, such an arrangement could brighten the home year-round.

THE ART OF ARRANGING

Large collections give owners an opportunity to experiment with placement. One popular option is to cluster a majority of the items together and set a few apart. An example of this can be seen in this display of beaded fruit. Most of the sparkling collectibles have been grouped in a wire basket, while six pineapples line up along the ledge. Not only does this kind of placement draw attention to variations in color and size, it also allows certain pieces to be chosen for their ability to coordinate with other prized possessions. For instance, the pineapples complement the hues of the landscape painting better than the other colors of fruit in the basket would have.

ABOVE: Bookshelves are some of the best places to display collections, as you can see with the antique china showcased in this sage-green living room. Pink lusterware is concentrated in the center of the built-in unit. The consistent handling of each shelf—three plates in the back and three items or small groupings in the front—achieves a clean, organized appearance. Although they are often overlooked, even the sides of shelves can be turned into display space. Here, smaller plates and saucers flank each shelf's central arrangement.

OPPOSITE: Humor can be a vital part of personalizing a room with collections. Alone, the stately cupboard with its well-presented grouping of brown-and-white transferware is an elegant addition to this great room (notice the generous amount of space each piece is given). With the extra touch of the large star propped on top, the cupboard more clearly conveys the unique vision of its owners. A star-motif lamp carries the star theme from ceiling to eye level. Silver treasures around the lamp base all mirror the pewter-hued finial positioned beneath the cupboard's central arch.

THE ART OF ARRANGING

OPPOSITE: How often do you spot single glasses at a flea market or yard sale? Most people pass them by, but this collector kept an eye out for examples bearing delicate etched designs. Arranged on an antique transferware platter, the grouping takes on the importance of a great collection. Similar displays can take shape with other mismatched items, such as teacups or saltshakers.

> ## good advice
> Small objects get lost in expansive settings. Choose a special display space— a curio cabinet or atop a toleware tray—to both highlight and protect them.

RIGHT: Large flat bowls are ideal spots to display collections of round objects. Even rag balls assume an air of elegance when placed in an antique wooden fruit bowl. Other items that might be arranged in a similar manner include vintage croquet or boccie balls, blown-glass Christmas tree ornaments, beaded-fruit oranges, and color-ful carpet balls. It's best to have a large enough selection to be able to line the bot-tom of the bowl and pile a few additional examples on top.

ABOVE: When a collection comprises items that are all of the same material and the same color, look for any variations that exist to determine the best display. The main difference among the alabaster treasures occupying this cabinet shelf is height: approximately half the items in the group are short, the other half are tall. Alternating short and tall designs across the span of the shelf creates a lively and eye-catching arrangement.

OPPOSITE: When determining placement within a tabletop display, it can often take time and considerable rearrangement of objects to settle on the best one. Look for similarities that might connect different pieces and then place those together. Group by size first. In general, taller pieces (even when the difference in height is minimal, as with these McCoy vases) look best in back to allow shorter ones to be seen. Next, analyze shapes. In the back row of this grouping, the vase with the round opening is flanked by two designs with square tops, creating subtle symmetry. Pattern can also link items to one another. Ribbed patterns unify the three vases on the far left, while scalloped tops can be seen on the two vases on the far right of the front row.

THE ART OF ARRANGING

ABOVE: Most home owners display possessions inside a cupboard; this collector opted for the top. Boxes give the back row of cream-colored McCoy vases added height. The oval mirror on the right introduces a different element to the all-pottery arrangement. To the left of the cupboard, strong vertical displays reinforce the lines of the tall piece of furniture. The plant stand between the suitcases and the cupboard makes an unexpected yet attractive support for additional vases.

THE ART OF ARRANGING

OPPOSITE: When one piece in a collection significantly dwarfs all the rest, make it the dominant element in a display and group the other pieces around it. In this folk art lover's living room, a commanding ship portrait hangs above an elegant dresser. Once this painting was in place, smaller examples were arranged around it. Frames of a similar width were hung down each side, two slightly bigger items were placed up above, and two diminutive designs occupy the lower right corner. The dresser-top display is kept simple to balance the busy look of the wall.

ABOVE: Layering a collection can sometimes be tricky when framed pieces and three-dimensional ones share the same space. The goal is to have each piece positioned so it can be seen clearly. Covering over a section of a frame or even a corner of the painting or print inside it is acceptable if doing so does not block the main image. The seascape at the center of this arrangement, for example, is visible even though portions of its ornate frame are hidden by the small print and the shadow-box ship model. Ample room is left between the shipping-related items on the table so that each can be viewed on its own while remaining part of the wider display.

LEFT: Determining the best display space for your possessions is sometimes half the battle of trying to create the perfect arrangement. Yellow McCoy pottery would look wonderful in just about any setting, but when grouped in a blue painted cupboard, the pieces shine even brighter. Variations in size and color are highlighted by mixing small, large, pale, and dark pieces on each shelf. Examples with particularly artistic patterns are situated toward the front of the shelf so that they can be clearly seen and fully appreciated.

OPPOSITE: Choosing a roomy cupboard as the receptacle for a large collection is wise for a number of reasons. For one, the multiple shelves provide ample room for display. Doors also allow owners the option of exposing their treasures or hiding them away when no one's at home. The owners of the colorful hand-painted pottery seen here chose to line the bottom shelves of the cupboard with similarly sized jars; they concentrated smaller pieces that might be difficult to see on a lower level on the upper shelves. With bright collections like this, pay attention to the movement of color within the space. A vertical row of yellow was created beginning with the teapot on the second shelf from the top. Other hues—the red, blue, and black in particular—move the eye around within the space.

THE ART OF ARRANGING

LEFT: A fun way to display figural collections is to mimic a natural setting. Loosely lined up on a wooden bench, for instance, these duck decoys seem to be casually floating on a pond. Other examples of this type of arrangement include the following: cement garden statuary (frogs, for example, or rabbits) clustered on the floor beneath a plant stand in a sunroom, snow babies playfully grouped on a snowy-white doily, or the skating figures from Lionel train sets positioned as if gliding across a tabletop mirror originally intended to hold perfume bottles on a vanity.

OPPOSITE: When working with many similar size objects, it is helpful to place some of the pieces up on a platform or pedestal. This arrangement of antique circus toys shows how many different kinds of platforms can be put to use. A clown and a horse-and-rider are propped in a long lidded box on the left, while another grouping stands on diminutive doll furniture (a bench, a footstool, and a small chair) on the right. Glass jars in the center of the table and a long box with drawers toward the back are also utilized.

LEFT: Creating the same number of groupings on each shelf of a bookcase or hutch is a good way to bring order to a varied collection. Here, antique baskets, boxes, prints, and painters' palettes harmonize perfectly. Each shelf contains three artful arrangements that are symmetrical but not identical. Up top, for instance, two smaller groupings flank a single strong element; notice the placement of the floral prints. Note, too, that larger pieces are placed on the lower shelves, while more intimate vignettes (containing multiple small objects that require closer inspection) are situated at eye level.

OPPOSITE: Towers are an excellent way to display items with flat tops and bottoms. This type of arrangement creates an imposing presence in an interior while highlighting subtle design variations in a collection. In this photograph, metal picnic baskets were stacked on a rustic bench. (The painted checkerboard floor pattern echoes the baskets' ocher hues.) A wood bucket was placed on top of one tower to match the height of the others; however, the single piece does not look out of place because its pronounced grain pattern resembles the faux-wood grain on a few of the metal boxes. Pantry boxes, hatboxes, and advertising tins are just a few of the objects that would also work well in towers.

OPPOSITE: Even when collections are clustered behind closed doors, care should be taken with regard to placement. That way, each time you go to retrieve an item, you are met with an organized (and pleasing) scene. This decorative tin and wood cupboard is home to numerous variations of Art Deco barware. Here, each category is concentrated on a shelf of its own. Moving up from the chrome ice buckets on the bottom shelf are chrome cocktail shakers, glass cocktail shakers and, finally, glasses and swizzle sticks on the top shelf.

RIGHT: In an uncluttered interior, a high shelf circling the room is a wonderful spot for simple displays. Vintage alarm clocks are lined up beneath the ceiling in this Arts and Crafts bungalow, providing a subtle hint of humor in the otherwise classic interior. Thoughtful placement prevents two similar colors or shapes from sitting directly next to one another. High perches are also advisable for displaying fragile collectibles in homes that have active children or pets.

BELOW: When hanging a large collection in a small space, pay attention to the different styles of frames—thick and thin, small and large, wood and metal, ornate and plain. Then alternate designs so that there is a balanced mix. This display of mirrors is a good example. Painting all the frames the same color (white in this case) is another way to prevent a sizable collection from overwhelming a room. The choice of deep olive walls beneath the white frames makes an attractive decorating statement.

ABOVE: Let similarities within a collection guide the order of a display. For example, the rippled edges of the two narrow mirrors make them a natural choice for the center of this dining-room arrangement. Two larger mirrors are situated on either side. The larger one hangs above a pretty plant stand that now holds antique decanters; the shorter shield design is better suited to the corner above a sideboard, so that fresh flower displays do not block the bottom of the mirror.

OPPOSITE: Ornate wrought-iron sconces and a pot rack become fine art when grouped on a wall. Although the forms vary slightly from one to another, the similar styling unifies the arrangement. When working with these items or others like them (salvaged fencing, for example, or pierced tin wares), consider the placement seen here. Anchor the display by hanging the largest item in the center of the space, suspend one smaller piece directly above the first, and then arch the remaining examples around either side.

THE ART OF ARRANGING

LEFT: Pyramid arrangements are ideal for collections of boxes—whether small boxes set on a tabletop or larger examples placed on the floor. Wonderful painted finishes unify the trunks and large boxes stacked in front of the window in this photograph. The base of the folk art bird sculpture adds a perfect finishing touch. Not only are box displays pleasing to the eye, they are also useful for storing table linens, board games, holiday decorations, and other items.

OPPOSITE: Runners provide an elegant foundation for displays on tables, dressers, sideboards, and other flat surfaces. The choice of color and material can complement both the room's décor and the objects in the collection. The graceful scalloped edge of this example echoes the curved candlestick and cut-glass pitcher up above. Although framed works of art are rarely layered so that one eclipses another, this home owner chose to do so in order to bring more depth to the overall arrangement. Recreating the still life with a trio of real pears is a playful touch; a similar effect can be achieved by pairing fresh flowers with floral still lifes.

THE ART OF ARRANGING

OPPOSITE: Simple rows of objects enhance pared-down interiors like this retro-style kitchen. Architectural stars stand above the sink, while enamelware coffeepots parade along the top of the vintage stove. The sole colored coffeepot was placed in the center and framed by the white examples. The butter-yellow enamel on the stove inspired the shade of paint on the walls.

RIGHT: A good way to handle a collection that consists of groups of similar items is by making distinct rows for each. Here, two rows of china canisters rest on a marble-top table. Because the items are fragile, the owner chose to display them behind a plush armchair. Placing collections slightly out of reach (as well as creating such a precise arrangement) sends a subtle message to guests that the pieces are not to be handled without asking. An embroidered tablecloth with a floral motif was framed and hung on the wall behind the display; the textile's scalloped edge echoes the delicate molded design on the canisters in the back row.

ABOVE: Imagine collections as paintbrushes and use them to add color to any part of a room. Examples of art pottery in creamy pastels and earth tones brighten a ledge in this yellow living room. Because so many color variations exist in the world of pottery (whites and creams, soft pastels, bold saturated hues), these pieces are especially well suited to the task. Regarding placement, an amateur still life forms the foundation of the arrangement. Balanced but asymmetrical groupings of vases sit on either side of the painting. The pink vase is intentionally set slightly apart from the pink frame in order to spread the color evenly.

OPPOSITE: Wall space is most often filled with one or more flat objects—frames, wooden signs, or textiles like hooked rugs. One creative home owner, however, chose an eclectic group of objects to adorn this corner of her living room. Beside an antique American flag (only two stripes are visible on the left side of this photograph) is an eye-catching display of patriotic items that includes framed prints, a painted wood shield, and parade flags propped up on high stands. Neutral, all-white details like the ceramic wall pocket vases and a light fixture originally intended for the ceiling add texture to the arrangement. To keep the varied collection from appearing chaotic, pieces fall loosely into two columns, one being the framed prints above the ceramic star and the other being the shield, fixture, and parade flags.

THE ART OF ARRANGING

OPPOSITE: Sepia tones unify a mixture of objects on display in a cupboard. Brown-and-white transferware is the dominant collection, but antique photographs, old books, and vintage note cards bearing fountain-pen ink that has faded to a deep brown are interspersed. On all three shelves, a row of flat pieces stands in the background (on the bottom shelf, the transferware bowl is flanked by pieces of architectural salvage). In front of those rows, three to four items are lovingly placed with plenty of space between each one. Unexpected touches add visual interest: the note cards, the photograph beneath the small cloche on the bottom shelf, and the coral and seashells filling the lidless serving dish on the top shelf.

ABOVE: Large collections can be shown in their entirety or can be arranged in smaller groups. If your style is to show everything at once, you'll need to maximize display space. In a cupboard or bookcase, that may mean propping up items against the back and the sides. Two additional ideas are offered here. Plates can be layered to fit a greater number on each shelf, while tiny hooks (available at hardware stores) can be attached to the front to support cups or creamers.

two

Decorating with Collections

Have you ever flipped through a mail-order catalogue or walked into a well-appointed hotel suite and noticed that even though the furnishings in the room are tasteful, the setting for some reason doesn't look lived in? You may not be able to put your finger on it, but something is clearly missing. That something is the accumulation and presentation of collections—the personal effects that make a house a home. The items with which we choose to surround ourselves tell the story of our lives: our interests and hobbies, where we've traveled, what artwork and graphic design appeal to us. Without them, interiors lack warmth, depth, and personality. In other words, they look like an image in a catalogue or a pallid room in a hotel.

PRECEDING PAGES: Sometimes collections act as the main source of color in an interior; other times they create a subtle secondary color scheme. Set in a sculptural built-in corner cupboard, blue-and-white spongeware adds unmistakable interest to this apple-green dining room and provides a pleasing echo of color with the blue-and-white weaving on the Shaker-style chairs. A single still life set between the cupboard and the doorway underscores the room's simple décor; an owner who favors a more abundant look might choose to hang a vertical row of images in the same place, like the three frames hanging in the sun-room (background).

OPPOSITE: When decorating a room in period style—whether late Victorian, Art Deco, or any style that tickles your fancy—displaying collections from the same era helps maintain the proper mood. Although this bedroom's antique furnishings call to mind our nation's early days all by themselves, the addition of baskets, period portraiture, a papered hatbox (under the high dresser), and blue-and-white Chinese porcelain drive the point home. Early American-style fabric was used to make curtains and a bed skirt. A number of paint, wallpaper, and fabric companies produce lines based on historic hues and patterns that can prove most useful in these pursuits.

Spaces need not be filled to the brim with priceless possessions to attain this desirable lived-in appearance. The number of objects on display and the manner in which they are arranged will depend greatly on the style of the décor and taste of the owner. When it comes to decorating their homes, most people fall into one of three groups. First, there are those who prefer a minimalist approach, opting for sleek furnishings, clean lines, and a few carefully selected pieces thoughtfully placed around the room. In the eyes of the second group, however, the pared-down look is slightly cold and impersonal. Instead, they are drawn to a style that might be better described as "over the top." Their favorite things spill from shelves and tabletops, cupboards, and windowsills; furniture, curtains, and carpeting often exude a similar exuberance. A third group falls somewhere in the middle of the previous two. These people generally favor a look that is homey yet not overcrowded; one that maintains a good balance between the number of possessions and the amount of display space at all times.

Which type of decorator are you? If you don't know the answer immediately, one good way of determining your natural nesting instinct is to sit down with a stack of home-design magazines and style books. Tear images you like from the magazines and mark pages you're drawn to in the books with sticky notes. When you've gone through the whole pile, see which type of interior you chose more often: Is it the clean-lined, white-walled space with a neat row of objects on a mantel? Or maybe it's the comfortable, sun-warmed keeping room with a stately hutch harboring cherished heirlooms and a quaint cluster of sepia photos adorning the wall. Or it might be the wonderfully quirky residence without an empty surface in sight—walls, tables, and ceiling beams covered from edge to edge with personal artifacts. Trust the evidence in front of you: the style that caught your eye with the greatest frequency is the one you'll feel most comfortable living with day after day.

In addition to the quantity of objects you feel at ease with, you may notice that one particular decorating style appeals to you more than others do. Did every page torn from a magazine "coincidentally" include a Scandinavian pattern or color scheme? Did you tend to skip over rooms that resembled an Adirondack cabin but find yourself pausing anywhere that honored the spirit of the Southwest? Keep track of all these preferences and delve deeper into any that really intrigue you. Perusing an entire book devoted to Southwestern style, for instance, might spark ideas about simple arrangements you can attempt on a kitchen counter or a bedside table, as well as display cupboards you might like to buy or have built for a certain room.

Once you've identified the look that is closest to your heart, you'll better understand where and how your collections can fit into the overall scheme.

While no hard and fast rules hold about what types of objects are appropriate for each room, some general guidelines can govern placement within a setting. As the most public room in the house, for instance, living rooms are wonderful areas to showcase objects that represent the interests of the entire family. Souvenirs from treks overseas and around the country—such as African masks or folk art from the American South—might be hung on the wall or lined up on a table. And a bookcase filled with antique leather-bound volumes on a topic you know intimately might spark conversations

Objects can be decorative and functional in the same setting, like the basket collection in this country living room. Small and medium designs are hung from nails in the exposed beam, displayed along the coffee table, and set on a chest below the sheep painting. Larger examples are placed on the floor where they hold items such as antique textiles (an American flag and patchwork quilts) and a flowering houseplant. Board games, firewood, and toys can also be stored in large baskets like these.

among your guests. Most living rooms are chock full of natural display spaces, such as mantels, coffee tables, bookcases, and desks, offering you plenty of options when it comes to placement.

Dining rooms, too, contain quite a few places that seem to call out for collections, like tall hutches, glass-front cabinets, and the wall space above sideboards. Collections related to dining are a natural fit here, whether they consist of grandmother's heirloom china, large groupings of brown-and-white transferware, or silver tea services in multiple patterns. Don't feel constrained, however, to stick to this particular theme if you have other inclinations. One gutsy couple who loves adventure travel and the great outdoors, for example, suspended a 1920s kayak above their sideboard; the visual parallel of the long table and the long boat seemed to fit perfectly within the otherwise traditional setting. Collections on themes other than dining can also be interspersed among plates and glassware, such as figurines, vintage postcards, or colorful tin wind-up toys meandering among the dishes on a cupboard shelf.

The kitchen is another room where food and cooking-themed collections are typically displayed. China, tin canisters, juice glasses, potato mashers, and wire whisks are just some of the items that look right at home. Many home owners choose to install open shelves—or to take doors off cabinets to attain open shelves—in order to highlight favorite objects. On the walls, traditional themes such as framed menus, illustrations from old cookbooks, and farm-stand signs advertising fresh eggs and produce are perfect choices. Untraditional images work well, too: landscape paintings, paint-by-numbers, or botanical prints of flowers or leaves. Kitchen collections are often grouped by color, such as a favorite Fiestaware hue. And sometimes a beloved animal theme makes its presence known throughout the space,

The decision to turn a solarium into a formal dining room allowed one collector to play with the garden themes she loves, including a small but eye-catching collection of baskets. Woodwork received a soft shade of sage green and a trailing ivy motif was painted along the top of the walls just below the ceiling. Matching garden urns were placed in the corners of the room to hold seasonal flowers, foliage, or evergreens. On a high shelf, four gathering baskets command attention. Tipping one design upwards and displaying another on its base as opposed to on its side keeps the arrangement lively.

OPPOSITE: One avid gardener relied on green-and-white collections to instill her bedroom with the spirit of the great outdoors. Sap buckets, botanical-motif boxes, and an architectural star are clustered on top of a whitewashed wardrobe with grass-green stripes. The wardrobe was slanted slightly away from the wall to soften the sharp angle of the corner. A woolen tulip-motif throw adorns the bottom of the bed; the pillow shams and lampshade up above were crafted from the surviving portions of a well-worn chenille bedcover. To create extra storage space in the small room, a ruffled skirt was attached to an old potting table with a faded green finish.

ABOVE: Many collections—like the vintage school items seen here—can be used to decorate children's rooms. Large maps can become learning tools and works of art when hung on the wall. Students once indicated the names of the states in chalk on this U.S. map. Note how the globe in the back has been placed on a stack of magazines to give it more visibility. Get your kids involved in choosing and positioning objects that interest them; having something of their own to look for will make antiquing as much fun for them as it is for you. Board games and lunch boxes from old television shows can be used as decorative elements in a child's room. Old sporting equipment like catchers' masks and tennis racquets can be arranged on a wall. And the wire baskets once used in locker rooms are great catchalls for toys, sneakers, umbrellas, and more.

as when a home owner who loves cows gathers pot holders, tea towels, dinnerware, and other accessories emblazoned with bovine motifs.

While there are exceptions to every rule, most home owners view bedrooms as sanctuaries from the worries of the world. As such, collections that are more private or soothing in appearance are frequently kept here. These might include Victorian perfume bottles, bud vases, frilly hats, gilded mirrors, and the like. Consider unexpected items as well, as long as they have a delicate, restful quality about them: Plates with attractive floral borders, for instance, look charming on the bedroom wall, as do ornate sections of salvaged fencing. This is one room in which natural display spaces may need to be supplemented, especially if alarm clocks, makeup, jewelry boxes, and other necessities are already crowding dresser tops, vanities, and bedside tables. A lovely hanging cupboard or small bookcase may provide enough added room; flat items can also be clustered on the wall above a bed or vanity or between two windows.

Additional, specialized display units are also a good idea for children's rooms, where some collections (like heirloom dolls, porcelain figurines, or vintage sports memorabilia) are best kept at a distance from items that can be played with on a regular basis. High shelves and glass-fronted cupboards are two good choices. Many storage options for children's rooms can work to complement collections on

display there. Locker room items are frequent finds at flea markets these days. Some examples include actual lockers painted in bright colors or wire baskets, both of which make appropriate holders for sports-related objects. Likewise, miniature doll chests garnered at flea markets, antiques shops, and thrift stores can be used in a little girl's room to hold doll clothes, stickers, or any number of things: lined up on a shelf, the containers become a collection unto themselves.

Anything displayed in the bath should be immune to moisture damage. This is less of a concern in powder rooms than it is in full baths with showers or tubs that can fill the room with humidity, though even in a powder room, the possibility of high humidity and moisture is always present. Furnishings, painted signs, or picture frames with weathered finishes, for example, will become excessively flaky over time in this kind of setting. Glass and china do nicely here, and one has many opportunities to put such collections to use here, as well. China vanity canisters and glass jars from barbershops or apothecaries can hold cotton balls, swabs, guest soaps, and bath oil beads. Ocean-themed items such as seashells or beach glass also fit in well. Small objects can be lined up along windowsills, backsplashes, and the ledges of beaded board; larger objects may need additional space, such as a glass-fronted apothecary cabinet or a series of short shelves hung on the wall.

Foyers and hallways can be handled in one of two ways. Either they can be repositories for extra pieces of a collection displayed in other rooms (thereby extending a particular theme throughout the house), or they can showcase a single collection unique unto itself. In the first scenario, a home owner who adores Flow Blue china may have a cupboard filled with dishes in the dining room, a basin and ewer set in the powder room, and a grid of four platters above her writing desk in the living room. In her foyer, she may choose to flank an elegant mirror with Flow Blue plates, effectively introducing guests to her passion as soon as they enter her home. Owners of many

OPPOSITE AND RIGHT: A willingness to blend old and new makes it possible to decorate an entire room with only a small or medium-size collection. Here, country antiques like the stuffed toys, patchwork quilt, and painted rope bed are combined with new textiles that evoke an old-fashioned feeling. Curtains made from reproduction homespun fabric hang at the window. A new blue-checked duvet and pillows covered with vintage-style ticking continue the blue-and-white theme on the bed. A hanging cabinet protects a collection of sheep toys. To give a sense of consistency to the group, all the sheep face the center.

different types of objects, on the other hand, may view the fact that hallways and foyers are removed from other rooms in the house as an opportunity to concentrate the entire contents of a collection there.

Offices and craft rooms are two other spaces within the home where collections can be a vital part of the décor. Since you will be working in this setting, items that spark ideas and revive the spirit are especially well suited. Displays related to the work that will be taking place there are also fitting. A writer might store a series of favorite childhood novels near the computer station, or frame dust jackets of beloved books and hang them on the wall. An advertising executive might store pens, paper clips, and various desktop supplies in tin kitchen canisters bearing the colorful vintage graphics of coffee, cookies, and other dry goods. An avid quilter might frame individual quilt blocks and arrange them in a grid pattern on the wall.

Using hues found in her collections, one home owner designed this graphic floor pattern for her hallway. The putty color also coats woodwork, while the stairs were painted brick red. Beaded-board paneling was applied to the ceiling and in an unusual direction—horizontally—along the walls. Antique game boards fill the wall beside the staircase; one cobalt-decorated crock stands on each step.

Now that we've learned a bit about what types of items fit well in particular settings, let's examine how to decide on placement within a room. Again, personal interpretation is always welcome. To begin, stand in the center of the room—be it a living room, kitchen, or bath—and analyze the space. Is your eye drawn to a particular focal point? Is there a mantel in the living room, open shelves flanking the stove in the kitchen, or a deep windowsill in the bath? If so, that is the first place to consider arranging a collection. If not, is there an open area that seems like a natural place to position a table, shelving unit, or display case? Depending on the size of your collections, a room may already have sufficient space to accommodate it all without overcrowding. If ample surfaces are lacking, however, you may decide to rotate your collections to display some while others are safely stored away.

A collection of paintings can enhance an interior without anyone having to hammer a single nail into the wall. Instead the frames can be propped against the wall on top of a mantel, sideboard, or bookcase. Two main placement options exist. First, the pieces can be lined up in a row; your own taste will dictate whether to set the frames close together or to leave ample breathing space between each one. The other option is to layer the images, like the rose still lifes seen here. When overlapping works of art, be sure not to block the main portion of the image.

ABOVE AND OPPOSITE: Spirited arrangements of vintage kitchenware help re-create the look of the house of the collector's grandmother. Stenciled patterns based on Pyrex mixing bowls were applied to existing cabinetry above the sink; on the opposite side of the room, a tall cupboard was painted jadeite green. The red on the walls matches the 1950s table (foreground). Next, the collections were put into place with an over-the-top approach. On the far wall, figural towel holders and hanging shelves lined with teapots and salt-and-pepper shakers fill every bit of available space. Period shelf edging enhances the overall look of the green cupboard.

Take a moment to judge the proportions of the room and the placement of windows as well. If ceilings are vaulted in your family room, for instance, but lower in the dining room, the former will probably be the best spot for large wall-mounted items; the latter will work best with cozy groupings on low surfaces. Likewise, if the living room features a grand bay window with a wide windowsill, that is arguably the best spot for a large arrangement of Murano glass—even if you originally thought to display it in a foyer lit only by the narrow transom of the door. (If you're absolutely set on using the foyer, track lighting can always be installed to supplement sunlight; see "A Look at Lighting" on page 140 for more information on this topic.)

One final thought regarding the room as a backdrop for your collections involves the colors and patterns that are or will be used to decorate the space. In some cases, home owners prefer that collections blend into their surroundings by becoming just one of the several elements that make up the whole décor. In other situations,

DECORATING WITH COLLECTIONS

they select collections for the primary burst of color or pattern in an otherwise neutral space. If a room is already decorated with deep salmon-colored walls and a dramatic cabbage-rose drapery fabric in pinks and greens, the collections displayed there would need to coordinate; green McCoy vases instead of cobalt ones, for example, or floral still lifes on the wall rather than monster-movie posters from the 1950s. By contrast, collections in all-white rooms can be positioned with the intention of adding color throughout the space—a cubby unit filled with red cast-iron fire engines, a long art shelf lined with cranberry glass, or a bookcase showcasing the sunflower-yellow bindings of National Geographic magazines. Possessions might even inspire a color for the walls or print for the furniture.

Once you have located the best room in your house and the optimal position within that space, there are a number of practical considerations. No matter how good your collections look, displays must ultimately allow for the normal functioning of a household. Bulky objects cannot block a high-traffic hallway, for example, while a sizable collection displayed on a desktop that the family uses regularly must leave ample room for a computer, telephone, writing surface, or other necessities. Then, when you've placed pieces where

SOUTH CHATHAM BOYS
IN SERVICE.
Charles E.H. Cahoon.
Randall H. Cahoon.
Ray S. Eldridge.
Albert L. Young.
Earl M. Allen.
Albert D. Barb
O. Stanley Eldri
Harry L. Youn
Robert L. Allen
Harrison I. Smal
rances Frazie
eorge F. Wad
orge W. Caho
erbert I. Macc
s B F d

ROOMS

OPPOSITE: Some collectors are drawn to a particular color, others to a certain material. The owners of this charming home appreciate a theme: anything with a patriotic motif. So large is their collection, that it forms the basis of the décor throughout the house. On their living-room mantel, framed American flags share space with assorted patriotic mementos such as the hand-painted sign honoring one town's soldiers from the Second World War. Walls are kept white to highlight the collections.

you think they look best, ask yourself the following questions. Do I still have unencumbered access to the things I'll need on a daily basis? (Porcelain animals set in front of antique books are less of a concern than those set in front of your address book, dictionary, or thesaurus.) Can I reach all the objects to dust them? Are fragile items set far enough away from the edges of tables, out of reach of children and pets? Attending to any issues at the time you put the items in place will prevent hassles—and possibly heartache—if something were to get damaged down the road.

When everything is in place, return to the center of the room and conduct a thorough aesthetic check of your surroundings. Be on the lookout for any table surface, shelf, or general area within the space that appears overcrowded. In each grouping, are any favorite pieces being hidden by larger objects? Might any tiny, uninteresting spots be enhanced by a beautiful vignette or intimate arrangement that will draw viewers near? Perhaps a gap remains on the wall or an empty surface you hadn't noticed before that is crying out for an artful selection of pretty things. Is there one place where the majority of color is concentrated, and if so, does it please your eye the way it is now? Maybe it would look better if a few of the most colorful objects were moved across the room to balance the look. When a final scan of the room leaves you fully satisfied, you'll know that each one of your possessions has found its proper home.

ABOVE: The area around a fireplace and mantel is a natural focal point in a room. Many people hang a single framed piece on the wall or line a group of eye-catching objects along the mantel. Another approach is illustrated here: The owner made the hearth the central point around which a large collection of needlework samplers is grouped. The warm red of the walls (a color reminiscent of the brick houses depicted on the samplers) is a good base for the framed pieces. If they were hung on a light-colored background, the numerous samplers might appear too busy.

ABOVE AND OPPOSITE: The theme of a collection can sometimes match the style of a house, such as Adirondack crafts in a cabin or Arts and Crafts pottery in a bungalow. In this seaside home, the living room's unusual double-shelf mantel displays collections relating to the beach. A row of vintage seaside postcards occupies the bottom shelf; up higher are a handful of seashells, an antique pail, and a selection of stars and moons. The rest of the room is kept clean and simple, with white walls and accent colors (pale blue, green, and peach) that look as though they popped off one of the vintage postcards.

BELOW: Knowing that his dining room would be home to collections of brown-and-white transferware and wooden doll chairs, the owner of this mountain hideaway applied bent twigs around the ceiling and doorways to emphasize the room's rustic theme. Tan paint on the walls was stained slightly to mimic age. The first element to be put in place in the wall display was the rustic mirror; plates were hung around it, and a table was placed under it. Positioning the diminutive chairs was the final step.

OPPOSITE: Bring a single piece of a collection (or a snapshot of it) with you when shopping for fabrics and paint colors to use in a room. The pottery that fills this stately corner cupboard inspired the choice of a black-and-white toile for upholstery and drapes. The wares also seemed to stand out well when set against a deep forest green, so the cupboard's interior was painted that hue. Black furnishings and white walls underscore the color scheme.

ABOVE: The focal point of this elegant kitchen is the generously proportioned range hood, where a salvaged portion of an old theater and a set of blue-and-white plates are prominently displayed. The plates also inspired the paint color of the room's wood paneling. Crown molding around the top of the room mirrors the styling of the hood. A plank of wood positioned above the stovetop adds another dash of ocher to the space; the four tiles and turkey-motif platter attached to it with wire clips can be taken down and used on the table during dinner parties.

Windowsill placement benefits pottery and glass because of the warm glow that sunlight bestows upon these materials. (Pottery and glass are also less susceptible to fading than other collections might be, such as antique toys, textiles, or books.) The wide surface of a bay window makes it particularly well suited to the task. Positioning a sofa in front of an arrangement like this is wise when working with fragile objects. Fabrics and furnishings in the room were selected to reflect the calming white-and-wood color scheme of this prominent display.

DECORATING WITH COLLECTIONS

decorator's tip

For years, decorators have known that layering crisp white slipcovers or lace-edged bed linens against an all-white backdrop instills a sense of serenity in any room. White-on-white collections add texture to these settings. You might arrange cream-colored porcelain figurines on top of a pretty lace doily or line up milk-glass candy dishes along a mantel. White McCoy vases fill this glass-fronted cupboard. Painting a cupboard's interior a warm shade of ecru can make bright-white collections stand out even more.

DECORATING WITH COLLECTIONS

OPPOSITE: Theme collections are perfect for open living/dining areas—especially in small dwellings—because they create a consistent look throughout the space. Garden antiques and botanical imagery personalize this converted hunting lodge. Prominent placement along the wide mantel raises everyday flowerpots to fine art; smaller examples are clustered on a table nearby. Confining this large collection of pots to only two surfaces keeps the look from getting too busy. Pressed leaves, flowers, and ferns were framed and hung on the walls. A soft blue was chosen for the walls to balance the dark woodwork and to add a hint of color to the predominantly earth-toned room.

ABOVE: This sunroom exhibits a number of good decorating ideas that will work anywhere in the house. A narrow table has been positioned behind the settee to support florists' baskets. (Vases, statuary, and wooden bowls are just a few of the other objects that can be placed on such a surface.) Mismatched fabrics on the wicker settee and chairs look perfect together because of their common floral theme. And the walls above the windows—usually an underutilized space—display pansy-motif paintings and prints. When choosing a paint color for the walls, find one that complements all the collections in a room; this moss-green paint is an ideal background for garden-related items.

decorator's tip

Removing objects from the settings they were originally meant for and displaying them elsewhere in the house can draw attention to sculptural qualities that may otherwise have been missed. These early-1900s mixing bowls are a perfect example. When arranged on a blue painted cupboard in the owner's foyer, their wide range of colors and molded motifs become more noticeable. Other possible combinations include colorful perfume bottles on a kitchen windowsill, silver-plate trophies on a dining-room hutch, and cast-iron toy trucks on a living-room mantel.

Positioning a small workstation in a living room, bedroom, or other space gives home owners yet another place to concentrate collections that inspire them. Here, a potting table has been transformed into a desk for a garden lover. Flowerpots, garden border tiles, birds' nests, and pheasant feathers discovered on country rambles are all concentrated in this blue painted piece. An antique bug catcher hangs from the drawer pull (when filled with sugar water, the clear glass jar lures insects and traps them). Artwork on the walls reminds the collector of her favorite four-footed friends. Stools are useful accessories to keep near a desk because they can support a stack of books or a cup of tea.

LEFT: To enhance a collection unified by its color scheme, one creative home owner decorated an entire room in bold red and green. Record album covers were used as templates for the squares of plaid and floral wallpapers that coat the upper walls and ceiling. Rich scarlet fabric with an old-fashioned rose pattern was chosen for the drapes. White beaded-board paneling and a whitewashed table keep the look grounded. Once the stage was set, a tabletop arrangement was made using red metal picnic baskets, a large red thermos, and a lamp with a decorative felt shade. Still lifes and serving trays with floral motifs were hung on the beaded board and up above on the wallpaper collage. An autumn foliage paint-by-numbers was given a bright red frame to coordinate with the other images.

OPPOSITE: Collections can blend into the background, or they can set the tone for an entire room. The latter is true of the dramatic display of floral still lifes hanging in this living room. The subject matter is the perfect counterpoint to the vintage bamboo furniture and bold floral fabrics that the owner loves. The brushstrokes on the paintings even inspired the mottled treatment of the walls. Other elements that continue the garden-friendly theme throughout the space include the weathered wood surfaces, the plentitude of baskets (including a lamp base), and the coffee table's cement urn planted with fresh flowers.

DECORATING WITH COLLECTIONS

ABOVE: There are many overlooked places in a house—the wall space between windows, for example, or the area behind a doorway like the one shown here. All can benefit from vignettes fashioned out of favorite collections. Simply position a small table or a stack of chests or baskets and hang a single framed image up above. Try to match the styling whenever possible; these trunks with attractive faux finishes and the framed needlework sampler both date back to the early 1800s.

DECORATING WITH COLLECTIONS

OPPOSITE: Proof that a few sculptural objects can create a strong decorative impact is presented in this bedroom vignette. Early-1900s dressmakers' mannequins (the one on the floor wears vintage bolo ties) and a small stack of vintage luggage add visual interest to the stately wardrobe standing at the center of the arrangement. An elegant piece of furniture like this wardrobe can act as the foundation for myriad displays: Position a single element beside it like a coatrack or salvaged pedestal, and place a row or cluster of objects up on top.

RIGHT: No home office should be without at least a few favorite pieces. Even the simplest display can trigger creative thoughts. Collections of containers (like these old metal toolboxes, and bread and document boxes) can also prove to be quite useful for storing office supplies. Other items well suited to a work space include anything related to the owner's career, like house models in an architect's studio, fountain pens on a writer's desk, or framed quilt blocks on the wall of a craft room. A work space like the one pictured here is easy to duplicate; simply place a desk in front of a wall of shelving. Concentrate books on upper shelves and keep the area directly behind the desk free for arrangements. A favorite painting hung in this unexpected backdrop can help rejuvenate a tired mind.

ABOVE: Fans of vintage kitchenware are often so passionate about their collections that they remove cabinets from their kitchens in order to display the objects in full view. Some opt for open shelves in place of cabinets, but these home owners arranged their enamelware, Pyrex, and scales on top of old kitchen furnishings and appliances. (People often appreciate old stoves when they spot them at flea markets but feel disinclined to restore them. Here's another way to use them.) White walls and pale gray woodwork and beaded-board paneling provide a neutral backdrop for the bright collections; the red chairs and floorboards provide a strong base for the colorful items up above.

OPPOSITE: Bright collections bring neutral settings to life. Solid-colored enamelware ewers are lined up along a stainless steel sideboard in this off-white dining room; filled with fresh flowers, the arrangement looks especially cheerful. Candy-colored glass goblets bring the same hues to the table. (The coordinating center-piece is easy to reproduce: Just place old-fashioned seltzer bottles and lemons on a silver tray.) To unify mismatched side chairs, the owners painted them the same glossy white as the table.
The corner cabinet's graceful scalloped edging frames a selection of ceramic bowls and reflects the curved forms of the chair backs. The shelves on which the yellow bowls are displayed have been painted a softer shade of the same color.

OPPOSITE: You've heard the saying, "Two are better than one"; in this sunny corner, a pair of collections proves the point. Yellow McCoy vases and painted furniture have been combined to create a stunning display. The majority of the vases are arranged in a blue bookcase (the combination of blue and yellow is a perennial favorite with decorators), while two additional vases are perched on top of a stack of small benches. Artful touches that finish the space include the botanical-print handbags on the bottom shelf of the bookcase, the 1930s floral prints on the striped walls, and a fern-embroidered pillow on the butter-yellow Windsor chair.

RIGHT: This elegant arrangement can enhance just about any setting and is easy to achieve. First, place a wide table beneath a sunny window and top it with favorite pieces of pottery. (Setting one smaller item on the windowsill draws the eye upward.) Next, add an element under the table; an old steamer trunk was used here, but a painted blanket chest or large vintage suitcase would work equally well. Finally, position a single graceful chair beside the table and hang a strong vertical painting, print, or photograph above it. In a setting that did not have beaded-board paneling on the walls, a column of three smaller images could replace the single framed piece.

DECORATING WITH COLLECTIONS

OPPOSITE AND RIGHT: Even the most serene interiors can harbor a kooky collection or two. In this pale-green bedroom filled with a few cherished photographs and furnishings, a coatrack set between the window and the doorway is an unexpected gathering place for colorful plastic bracelets. Graceful bowls are also good places to concentrate fun collections in serious settings (fill one with marbles, sea glass, or Cracker Jack prizes).

OPPOSITE: One of the first things to do when decorating with collections is to locate the room's natural focal point. In the airy living room of this lakefront retreat, it is the wall directly above the fireplace. Therefore, the tallest model boat in the owners' collection was positioned there. Other examples are scattered around the room, among them two motorboats on the mantel directly below and another sailboat on a chest in front of the windows. Walls and upholstery fabric are bright white, allowing the collections to take center stage.

RIGHT: A selection of school clocks from the 1920s hangs in the hallway of this collector's home. None tells the correct time, but the strong graphics and aged finishes make them well suited to an artful arrangement on a wall. The other furnishings in the hallway and the room beyond (including the small table, gumball machine, and salvaged lamp bases) also possess worn surfaces and a slightly quirky quality, making them good counterparts to the clocks.

DECORATING WITH COLLECTIONS

OPPOSITE: Doorknobs were screwed into the walls of this master bath to support a collection of vintage mirrors. The reflective surfaces are ideal for the setting; not only do they brighten the space—they also ensure that passersby won't have a hair out of place. Galvanized metal toolboxes hold washcloths, toilet tissue, soaps, and other bath necessities.

ABOVE: Which collections are appropriate for decorating a bath? With the exception of rare antiques or artwork that could be damaged by moisture, there are no limits on what can be used. This home owner chose a mixture of traditional and untraditional items. Mirrors with dark-wood frames grace the walls, while art pottery vases fill the dry sink. The warm pumpkin-colored walls complement the dark wood of the furniture and the mirrors. A wing chair and Oriental carpets add luxurious touches to the spacious room.

LEFT AND OPPOSITE: When decorating a bedroom, choose favorite objects and themes to create a special sanctuary. Dog portraits discovered at flea markets, green Floraline pottery from the 1950s, and antique books with rich gilded leather bindings are beloved by the owners of this interior. To recreate the look in your own home, start with a dramatic bed frame flanked by open shelves. (A pair of freestanding bookcases will do if built-in designs like these are not an option.) Hang a single piece of artwork over the bed and a column of other examples nearby. Fill the shelves with lively but not overly crowded arrangements. Painting the ceiling the same color as the walls makes even the most spacious room feel cozier.

good advice

Can't decide whether to create streamlined displays or ones that overflow? Scan decorating magazines to see which style catches your eye most often.

DECORATING WITH COLLECTIONS

OPPOSITE: Large collections are often the dominant decorating force in a room. Clear-glass cake stands make a strong statement in this dining room. The owners' decision to divide the collection between two shelving units was a good one: If it had been displayed across the entire wall, the grouping would likely have been too much to take in all at once. The narrow strip of sage green with its trio of brown-and-white transferware plates offers the eye a place to rest. A crystal chandelier was a perfect choice here since it echoes the look of the room's collection.

RIGHT: Ordinarily, small rooms get easily overcrowded when populated with too many furnishings or oversized pieces. Combining whitewashed finishes with all-white collections is one way to prevent this from happening. This cottage dining room is a good example. Though its proportions are decidedly cozy, a massive hutch filled with white ironstone looks right at home. Neat rows of plates and platters keep the large collection under control; most of the pitchers are concentrated on lower shelves, but a select few add dimension to upper shelves. White enamelware is clustered up top. (A willingness to accept small chips in the enamel coating allows enthusiasts to build up lively collections quickly and inexpensively.) White wicker garden furniture, decorative white metal sconces, and a sheer white curtain at the window also blend into the setting without overwhelming it.

OPPOSITE: Even the coziest corner in a home can benefit from collections. Wood frames hung against a stark white background enliven this cottage's sunny reading area. Because the space is so small, empty frames work best: If each were filled with a painting or print, the result would be an overcrowded look. Two framed prints propped up against the wall on the floor add a casual touch to the space. Sheathed in ocean-blue slipcovers, the chair and ottoman add color to the scene. A coordinating patchwork quilt is an ideal accessory for chilly evenings. Vacation-home touches include the fishing poles behind the chair, the fish above the doorway, and the vintage globe underneath the craft table.

ABOVE: A set of forty pressed-leaf designs creates a memorable wall treatment in this nature lover's bedroom. The precise grid pattern achieves a graphic look that does not overwhelm the space. Simple sheets of glass and art clips (available in art-supply stores) are an affordable alternative to framing. The soft ocher walls complement the sepia tones of the dried leaves. Other garden-inspired details in the room include the painted bench beside the bed, the rose-patterned duvet and pillow sham, and the whitewashed porch chair in the corner. A rustic branch secured above the window supports a sheer curtain and provides a perfect finishing touch.

OPPOSITE: This vignette demonstrates how easy it is to bring Early American style to any dwelling, even a modern one (a good thing when one spouse loves country decorating while the other favors a more contemporary look). First, set the stage by positioning a dresser and hanging shelf in a room; both should be the same color, either a warm wood stain or a painted finish like the deep gray seen here. Next, arrange folk-art objects in a pared-down manner. Rag balls in neutral tones fill the shelves; on the dresser, a horse pull toy, painted box, and black rag balls are carefully placed on a hooked rug. The styling of the collections conveys a country sensibility. What makes the look fresh and modern is the simplicity of the arrangement.

RIGHT: Collections often inspire the paint color in a room; this grouping of white-washed finials determined the choice of wallpaper. Furnishings and accessories like the metal table, clock frame, and mirrored Art Deco bed frame echo the wallpaper's charcoal gray urn pattern. Floorboards received a dramatic dark stain that complements the gray of the walls. Windows were left curtainless to emphasize the interior's clean lines and strong architectural elements.

DECORATING WITH COLLECTIONS

OPPOSITE: A love of horses inspired the decorating direction of this country bedroom. The decision to position the beds with the canopied headboards facing the doorway leaves the far wall free for arranging artwork, statuary, and accessories. The canopies also form an arch that beckons guests to step inside. Because it can be difficult to find antique quilts that match, the owner chose two examples with a similar green-and-white color scheme. The green hue inspired the paint on the woodwork, which complements the sunny yellow of the walls. Floors and bed frames are left unadorned and other furnishings in the room are minimal (only a chair, peg rail, and mirror) to focus full attention on the collection.

RIGHT: Set against this bedroom's creamy white walls, a mixture of items in warm browns and tans evokes the atmosphere of a bygone era. The vintage suitcases stacked at the foot of the bed are not only attractive, but also provide valuable storage space for bed linens, photographs, writing paper, and other sundries. A tower of toiletry cases supports a potted orchid against the wall, while three wooden boxes on the bedside table carry the stacking theme throughout the room. Folded quilts in a large basket on the floor pick up the faded rose hue visible in the vintage botanical prints and paintings. Placing the floral still life on top of the wall's sculptural architectural element creates an energetic play of great and small. As a thoughtful placement in front of the square, a well-aged floral print transforms the salvaged porch posts and mannequin into works of art.

LEFT: Arranged along a wall of shelves, collections become a decorative element, and set the tone of an entire room. Lu-Ray pastels allowed this collector to decorate her living room with the soft hues she adores. Thoughtful placement creates a look that is abundant but not cluttered. A good amount of breathing room is left between pitchers and teapots; a single teacup or set of salt-and-pepper shakers breaks up long lines of plates and platters. Plush pillows covered with vintage fabrics reflect the colors up above. Drastically different results could have been achieved if Fiestaware, white McCoy vases, or blue-and-white sponge-ware pitchers were used in place of the Lu-Ray. No matter what a person's favorite color scheme is, there exists a collection that can bring it to the forefront in an interior.

OPPOSITE: A love of kitchenware from the mid-1900s inspired this colorful décor. The bold yellow of the kitchen walls and the deep teal green of the mudroom beyond were matched to favorite pieces of pottery (notice the yellow pitcher on top of the red shelving unit and the green bowl and pitcher on the countertop on the right). Linoleum remnants were pieced together to form the dazzling floor pattern. The owner's creative touch can also be seen in painted details around the space: she sponge-decorated the two small hanging shelves on the left, mimicked a cow motif on the high shelf above the sink, and added a cheerful touch to the woodwork surrounding the back door. Even the cabinets were given a touch of color using vintage knobs and drawer pulls.

three

Making Objects Look Their Best

ALTHOUGH COLLECTIONS CAN MAKE A ROOM COME TO LIFE, THEY can also get lost in the shuffle of furniture, accessories, and everyday items. To make your possessions stand out as they should, certain factors must be in place: proper lighting is one necessity; ample display space is another. Without essential elements like these, your arrangements may never achieve their full decorating potential. In this chapter we discuss the special needs and finishing touches that will ensure that your favorite things always look their best.

PRECEDING PAGES: Track lighting enhances collections because it can be positioned precisely where you need it, whether you want to focus on a single favorite piece or illuminate a group of objects. Here, two lights are trained on a large painting. The wall unit next to the painting demonstrates how bookcases can accommodate any type of object, from model houses to stacks of quilts.

OPPOSITE: Custom display units can be anything you envision, from a wall of cubbies to a salvaged column reinvented as a pedestal. Here, two shelves have been built near a sunny window, one on the same level as the windowsill and another about a foot below. Paintings are propped up on the narrow upper shelf; vases with sculptural silhouettes are lined up below.

custom display units

When arranged on shelves or other types of units designed specifically for display, large groupings assume added importance and become the focal points of an interior. There are several situations in which this option should be considered. For example, if a room's existing shelves and tabletops are not sufficient to hold all the items in an arrangement (either because the collection is too big or the room too small), then additional, specialized display space would be a great help. Custom units can also solve the problem of how to showcase objects that are visually interesting on all sides and should therefore be viewed from both front and back.

In terms of planning and installation, shelving is the simplest of all custom-display options. A room may have an obvious niche that calls out for additional shelves (an alcove, for instance, or a short wall against which none of your furniture looks quite right). Spacious interiors can accommodate shelves that occupy a full wall, floor to ceiling, while interiors that are somewhat cramped may require only one or two art shelves hung above a desk, or a narrow shelf close to the ceiling that runs the length of one wall or around the entire room. In terms of design choices, shelves can be made of wood or transparent glass or Plexiglas, which looks especially nice in front of a window supporting a collection of colored glass.

Cubbies constructed from wood, Plexiglas, or another material are an additional option that provides home owners with numerous display possibilities. Set in their own compartments, cherished items can be viewed individually yet still come across as a cohesive whole. These tiny units can be set flat against the wall or can be designed as a freestanding piece that performs double duty as a room divider. Freestanding cubbies are perfect for items that should be viewed from both sides, such as vintage lunch boxes abounding in colorful graphics. Additional design options include painting or wallpapering the insides of each square or rectangular cubby to complement colors or furnishings found elsewhere in the room.

A third choice for custom display units consists of the one-of-a-kind pieces that can be found at flea markets. One possibility might be a bank of open letter boxes salvaged from an old post office or hotel front desk. One creative person even transformed the backs of two church pews into wall-mounted supports for a collection of white ironstone platters. To find the materials needed for all the decorating schemes mentioned here, do-it-yourselfers can head to their local hardware store, lumberyard, or home improvement outlet; less handy folks should enlist the aid of a carpenter.

MAKING OBJECTS LOOK THEIR BEST

OPPOSITE AND RIGHT: This wonderfully quirky kitchen demonstrates just how one-of-a-kind custom display units can be. In the tall cabinet beside the table, shelves support stacks of vintage tablecloths and colorful chintzware plates; a glass door keeps dust away from these cherished collections. Cubbies near a window accommodate tea towels and favorite pieces of pottery as well as narrow drawers filled with utensils, matchbooks, and other kitchen necessities.

MAKING OBJECTS LOOK THEIR BEST

an artful ledge

A ledge may be short or long, narrow or wide—but no matter what its dimensions, this type of surface seems to call out for the display of collectibles. Depending on a particular ledge's size and setting, it may even be the perfect spot for a particular kind of object. For instance, it may never have occurred to you to use the top of wainscoting for display, but miniature items can look wonderful on these narrowest of ledges. Collections related to water, such as seashells, starfish, or beach stones look especially attractive in a bathroom. Vintage menus or matchbooks, on the other hand, might work well in a dining room or kitchen. And old-fashioned postcards or Victorian tintype photographs could easily parade along a hallway's wainscoting.

Wider ledges like mantels and deep windowsills allow collectors greater flexibility when it comes to arrangements. Objects here can be layered a bit. To keep all possessions in view on interior ledges, lean flat or larger items against the wall in the back (framed photographs or antique platters, for example), then place medium-size objects such as vases or statuary in the center, and put smaller pieces like vintage wind-up toys or silver napkin rings up front. Find the best placement for the largest or heaviest pieces first to establish a foundation, then play with smaller items until the balance is just right. Keep windowsill displays simple: set a single row of objects going across, or concentrate a small grouping to one side. By not cluttering the space, you maximize the sunlight on the collections and in the room.

OPPOSITE: The narrow ledge above the wainscoting in this master bath supports a casual row of surf-smoothed stones. Other tiny collections that would look great in a similar setting include seashells, beach glass, and vintage postcards of seaside destinations. Always leave ample space between small items on a ledge so that the individual characteristics of each can be appreciated.

BELOW: High ledges obscure portions of objects from view, so anything placed there should be tall, colorful, or sculptural enough to be seen from below. Even though these vintage oilcans are set above eye level, the wide range of heights and designs is visible to everyone in the room.

Narrow ledges accommodate picture frames quite nicely. In this study, family portraits, engravings, and art photographs span the length of one wall. A second layer of frames rests on a writing desk beneath a large mirror. To keep the arrangement from looking cluttered, furnishings and artwork that share the space are kept simple.

MAKING OBJECTS LOOK THEIR BEST

A wide ledge above a room's wainscoting offers collectors another surface on which they can play with placement. This vignette could be recreated in any room. Begin with a single side chair set against the wall. Above it, layer three favorite images that have been framed in a similar fashion. Choose two small items to put on either side of the frames; to continue the layering effect, position each piece so that it overlaps the frames slightly. As a finishing touch, flank two taller possessions on either side of the arrangement.

good advice
When you take artwork to a framer, bring snapshots of your rooms. They'll help you determine what kinds of frames are appropriate.

arranging frames

A large, open wall is one of the most daunting sights in interior design. Home owners sometimes feel that they must find a single painting or object to fill the space, and very often the wall stays bare for months or even years while the search is under way. Fortunately, hanging multiple framed images is one of the easiest and most stylish ways to triumph over this tricky situation. Frames can be placed in a symmetrical grid, mirroring orderly displays found elsewhere in the room, or they can be arranged in a more haphazard manner—expressing a casual chic style that guests are sure to admire.

The first decision to make is what to hang. Some popular choices are botanical prints, historical engravings, black-and-white photography, and family portraits representing many generations or just one (all kids, for example). When you've identified the most appropriate images for a particular room, the next thing to consider are frames. By and large, arrangements look most cohesive when the frames are either identical or show variations on a theme (like all mahogany frames that range subtly in size and style). Your selection of frames can also become a decorative element in the room. Thick black frames are especially attractive in modern interiors, whereas whitewashed or ornate silver frames evoke a more old-fashioned feeling.

BELOW: Paintings, photographs, and prints are among the most common images to be framed and arranged on a wall, but many other options exist. In this sunny kitchen, menus from the owners' travels have been hung in a row above the cabinets. Matching frames unify the collection.

OPPOSITE: The size of a cluster of frames should be flexible. It can be concentrated over a small desk or chair, or it can expand to fill an entire wall. The manner in which the frames are hung can also vary. Precise grids complement simple interiors, while loose displays blend nicely with country décors. To create a loose arrangement similar to the one seen here, start with a single image and add others by eye without the aid of templates or a level. The space between frames may not be the same all around, but that only accentuates the casual appearance.

decorator's tip

Framing is an easy way to transform ordinary images into works of art. For example, posters or postcards of famous paintings, prints, or photographs can look like the real thing when surrounded by a beautiful frame. In the garden lover's living room shown here, scrapbook pages adorned with pressed leaves were framed and hung in a tight grid pattern. Keep an eye out for tattered books at flea markets and thrift shops; illustrations suitable for framing can often be found in these inexpensive volumes.

Once you have chosen the artwork and frames, a new question arises: How best to arrange the frames in the space allotted? The answer to this may depend upon the size and shape of the images themselves. If they are all the same size and are finished in a similar way—such as a set of four botanical prints surrounded by delicate gold frames—then a simple row or grid will be most pleasing to the eye. If, however, each work is a different size and shape (as is often the case with family photographs), then a more random placement that varies horizontal and vertical images will probably work better.

To find the best layout, create paper templates to represent each frame and arranging them either on the floor or directly on the wall using nonstaining art putty (available in art supply stores).

Always keep at least three to four inches between each frame to avoid a look that is too crowded. When working with different size frames, consider choosing one image or a similarly scaled pair for the center to anchor the overall plan, then maintain a certain degree of symmetry on either side to keep the overall look balanced. For example, you might choose to flank your anchor artworks with three small frames on the right and two medium frames on the left. The center of any row, grid, or arrangement should be at eye level.

Once you find a plan you like, using a pencil (pens and markers can permanently stain paint or wallpaper) make light marks on the walls where each frame should go. Because all frames are usually hung straight regardless of arrangement, add a level to your list of installation necessities; other must-haves include a hammer, nails, and picture hooks—all available at hardware stores. A stepladder can prove handy as well. Invite a spouse or friend to assist in the hanging process to act as a second set of hands and eyes.

A single row is one of the simplest arrangements that can be presented with frames. When positioned above a line of chairs like these, a set of images (pressed ferns in this case) can create an artful vignette in any room. Matching frames attain a cohesive look. When combining frames and chairs, there are endless design options to try. They might all be the same color, like the whitewashed examples seen here. Or you can mix and match: gold frames over white chairs, black frames over gold chairs, mahogany frames over red chairs. The choice is up to you.

One way to tackle a large expanse of empty wall space is to hang a collection of plates. Arrangements need not be made up of antiques or single-themed plates exclusively; this hallway showcases plates covering many dates and styles. For collections that are still growing, leave plenty of space among dishes and then fill in the gaps as new pieces come along.

good advice

To keep arrangements of large collections looking fresh, rotate items in and out of storage. Doing so will also prevent overexposure to sunlight, dust, and accidental damage.

hanging plates and platters

In recent years, it has become increasingly common to hang decorative plates and platters on the walls. The unexpected placement draws attention to intricate patterns and subtle hues to be found on the ware and adds a fresh look to a room. Some people are inspired to hang a selection of similarly colored plates; they may be drawn to the soft tones of brown-and-white transferware or the dramatic cobalt patterns of Flow Blue. When creating an arrangement, others opt for a particular design—many variations of the rose pattern are particularly popular. Ironstone platters are another common choice since the sculptural pieces look equally attractive in all-white rooms and when set against a colorful background.

When hanging plates and platters many of the same principles apply as for hanging frames. The first step in the process is finding proper hanging supplies, available at most art supply or hardware stores; be sure to jot down the dimensions and weights of large pieces so you will get holders strong enough to support them. Next, create paper templates to plan out their placement in the same manner as when hanging frames. A single row of plates can be hung either horizontally or vertically (vertical rows of plates are especially well suited to the narrow wall space between doorways and windows). Grids of plates or platters assume a formal feeling when arranged over a sideboard or writing desk, and all-over patterns instill a lively look and are a good format for displaying a large collection of plates. Because of the size of the pieces, filling a wall with platters could overwhelm small spaces, so always take room dimensions into account when planning an arrangement.

Arrangements of plates can be manipulated to fit any wall space in a dwelling—large rectangles over a mantel, narrow columns between windows, even triangles beneath a staircase. To create the display seen here, three blue-and-white plates were first hung at an angle that parallels the stairs; three more designs were then positioned to form a right angle.

LEFT: The wall space over a doorway or window is a good spot for a single row of plates. To center the arrangement, jot down the dimensions of the window or doorframe and the diameters of the dishes. Then figure out a plan that leaves an even amount of space from both each edge as well as between each plate.

OPPOSITE: A vertical row of three plates enlivens narrow spaces between doorways and windows. When positioned above a favorite chair, it also creates a decorator-perfect vignette in any room in the house. The three plates can have the same pattern or color scheme, or they can simply resemble one another in style. Reducing the size of the plates as the eye moves from bottom to top achieves a pleasing look.

MAKING OBJECTS LOOK THEIR BEST

A corner in a dining room, kitchen, or pantry is the perfect place for installing open shelves like these. Consider unexpected paint colors that will complement your collections, like the soft olive against which a large collection of yellowware mixing bowls are arranged. Bring a snapshot or a small piece from a collection to a paint store and hold swatches against it until you find a good match.

a look at lighting

In conjunction with placement, lighting can make or break the look of a collection. Just as you wouldn't think of setting a taller object in front of a shorter one, thereby blocking the latter from view, so too, should you avoid positioning a lovely grouping of antiques in a dark corner. To do so would be to negate all the time and effort you'd invested in gathering and arranging. When done correctly, lighting should not stand out; instead, the focus of attention should be on the collection itself.

To begin, you will need to assess a room's natural light. If a space has large windows that let in abundant sunlight, most collections can stand alone without additional lighting throughout the course of the day. While this is the case in many houses, dark apartments and north-facing rooms may need added illumination. The solution may be as simple as setting a lamp beside a tabletop filled with paperweights or garden statuary. Installing track lighting overhead can also be used to bring out the best in a collection.

Lamps or track lighting that enhance an arrangement in a dark room or on a cloudy day will likely be just as useful once the sun goes down. Track lighting can be especially dramatic when used to highlight a single item or series of related items placed around the room, such as curvaceous sculptures or architectural elements. When directed in this manner, the look is reminiscent of an art gallery and therefore conveys a heightened degree of importance to whatever falls under the spotlight. In fact, it can be helpful for home owners to visit a local museum, gallery, or historic house for inspiration. If you call ahead to determine a convenient time, a curator or docent may even be able to lead you through the space and point out how lighting has been used to enhance the exhibition.

Other forms of localized lighting can help bring collections to the forefront of a decorating scheme. For example, paintings, posters, prints, and photographs often benefit from a small lamp installed directly above them on the wall. The size and style of the lamp will depend on what is set beneath it. These types of lights not only help draw the eye to favorite images, but they also subtly brighten the area of the room they inhabit. To enhance denser groupings of art, pottery, figurines, vintage toys, or heirloom china, cupboards and bookcases can be wired with small lights set out of sight on the underside of the shelves. This solution works particularly well with arrangements that are set in deep cupboards, where items placed toward the back are often lost in the shadows.

MAKING OBJECTS LOOK THEIR BEST

Installing lights inside a cabinet ensures that the collections on display will be seen at their best. Two main options exist. One is a single row of lights above the top shelf, like the example in this dining room. The other involves installing a small light under each shelf. When working with a single row of lights, it can be helpful to leave open space between the shelves and the back of the cupboard so that light can travel from top to bottom. An added benefit of this open space is that tall items like this game board can be propped up behind the shelves.

LEFT: Bright sunlight enhances objects with ornate molded designs, like the white ceramic pieces seen here. Arrange such objects on a windowsill or table near a sunny window to achieve a similar effect. A textural tablecloth or runner used as a foundation will also benefit from natural light.

OPPOSITE: Kitchen windowsills are popular places to display collections of glass. Cobalt bottles in a variety of sizes and shapes grace this sunny spot; bottles can also be used to hold fresh flowers from the garden. Other categories that would look great here include cranberry glass, Depression glass, and Carnival glass.

care and cleaning

Proper care can make a world of difference when displaying collections. Not only will it protect the value of your possessions, but it will ensure the condition of the items in years to come. Many collectors view themselves not as owners of these objects but as caretakers so that future generations can enjoy them as well. Knowing what to do and how much attention should be paid to each piece is key.

Dust is one of the biggest enemies of anything on display. Home owners who abhor regular dusting would be wise to display their collections behind glass. Others should set up a cleaning schedule. For optimal results, dusting once per week is best, with gaps between sessions not exceeding a month. It should include items placed on high shelves that are all too often overlooked, except perhaps during spring cleaning and house spruce-ups around the holidays.

Regular dusting is also necessary for furniture and, many conservators feel, is all it requires in terms of routine care. The many brands of furniture polish on the market today, these same experts claim, do more to make the home owner feel good than they do to improve the overall condition of the furniture. So keep the use of waxes or sprays to a minimum. For the metals in your home—silver, brass, copper, pewter—two to three times a year is also a good schedule for checking and, if need be, cleaning and polishing them. Over the years, excessive polishing can wear down intricate engraved patterns.

Because textiles are prone to attack by insects and mice, it's a good idea to examine them at least every three months. Shake them out, inspect closely, and vacuum accumulated dust with a brush attachment. If the fabric or stitching is extremely delicate, vacuum through a fine mesh screen available at hardware stores (tape over sharp edges before proceeding, to protect both the textile and your fingers). Unless the items in question are tablecloths that are used on a regular basis, washing with soap and water should be infrequent, as repeated stimulation can damage delicate fibers and needlework. If it's absolutely necessary, hand wash all but the sturdiest textiles (like strong cotton or linen tablecloths, napkins, and runners, which do fine in the machine's gentle cycle) in cool water and mild detergent. Rinse well and dry flat.

Final words of advice: When checking on objects throughout the year, take time to consider any elements in the room that may have changed since you first settled on the arrangements. For instance, sunlight may shift from one part of a room to another as seasons change, and most precious objects should be kept out of direct sunlight.

ABOVE: Small stands or easels intended for frames (available in art supply stores or frame shops) can also be used to prop up plates and platters. For the most cohesive look, choose the same style of easel for each item in your collection.

OPPOSITE: Large displays on open shelves look stunning in an interior, but to keep them looking their best involves a serious commitment to cleaning. Regular dusting is a necessity. Dust is one of the major culprits when collections appear to lose their sparkle. Though it may seem daunting, setting up a regular cleaning schedule need not be overwhelming. You might start with a weekly once-over with a feather duster or lightweight dust-absorbing wand (available in supermarkets and home-accessory stores). Several times a year, remove the items from the shelves to vacuum out the corners. This can be a good time to rearrange your possessions or rotate new items into the display to keep the look fresh.

Painting the inside of a cabinet or cubby an unexpected color can make the collections on display really command attention. A deep red was chosen for the interior of this glass-fronted cabinet; the hue imparts a warm glow to the silver tea services and accessories on the shelves.

MAKING OBJECTS LOOK THEIR BEST

decorator's tip

Proper storage is essential to the longevity of your collections. The first consideration is how to pack away objects safely. Archival materials like acid-free boxes and tissue (available at art supply stores) are a must. Next, find the most suitable storage space in your home. Experts advise closets or cupboards in the main living area of the house where temperature and humidity levels are relatively stable. Attics and basements are acceptable only when they are climate controlled; in basements, always place boxes on shelves or palettes in case of flooding.

OPPOSITE: If planning an entire wall unit in which to display a collection, consider leaving the center open to create a banquette. In dining rooms and breakfast areas, a table can be placed in front of the additional seating; in living rooms and bedrooms, the spot can become a favorite place for reading or quiet contemplation. The open space also becomes a natural spot for a single, striking work of art.

BELOW: Sometimes all that's needed to create custom display units is to slightly alter a room's existing cupboards, cabinets, or bookcases. The owners of this home removed the doors from their kitchen cabinets, exposing open shelves on which vintage tins, trays, and green pottery are now arranged.

ABOVE: Hallways often have large expanses of wall space that can accommodate custom display units. Toy motorboats fill cubbies in this all-white space. Model sailboats rest up top and along a ledge nearby. Related artwork like the motorboat print, visible on the left side of this photograph, enhances a theme collection such as this.

OPPOSITE: Hanging shelves of this design can often be found at flea markets; a fresh coat of paint can match any shade of paint on walls or woodwork. When arrangements are made up of objects that are all the same hue, consider an accent color and use it generously around the room. In this kitchen, the vintage wares and the walls are green; an accent color of red can be seen in the curtains, carpet, seat cushion, and small pitcher. The red dining room in the foreground carries the color throughout the house.

RIGHT: A number of unexpected display units are found in this bedroom vignette. First, a hanging cabinet beside the window holds a vase and a figurine and supports a painting in an ornate gold frame. Above the bed, three display shelves in varying colors each showcase a single item. Chairs can be used as pedestals, too, as this weathered side chair attests. When browsing through flea markets, train your eye to spot potential in objects that might not seem right at first. All the pieces shown here complement the owners' preference for pale green; in your own home, the same pieces could be repainted in your favorite shades.

MAKING OBJECTS LOOK THEIR BEST

MAKING OBJECTS LOOK THEIR BEST

OPPOSITE, LEFT: The wall beside a staircase is an ideal spot to hang old family photos. To keep the arrangement from looking too busy, the owners brought their heirloom snapshots to a frame shop and chose one consistent style—white matte board and gold frames for each one. Two exceptions were matted years ago in brown; these were hung far apart to allow the color to be spread around. Creating a similar arrangement takes planning. Paper templates or a rough sketch on graph paper will help lay out the overall scheme before a single nail is driven into the wall.

OPPOSITE, RIGHT: Rustic frames complement the décor of this foyer. Natural history prints and green matte boards were both good choices for a space dominated by green woodwork and leaf-motif wallpaper. The largest frame in the group was fitted with a mIrror and hung over a hall table, acting as the central point around which smaller frames are clustered. An added benefit is the fact that the mirror hangs opposite the front door: The tableau reflects the trees outside and therefore enhances the botanical theme indoors.

RIGHT: If several framed images in a collection are similar to each other, break up the group and spread it around the display. In this hallway, four American flags are interspersed with single stars and a star-and-quilt block montage. Hanging the smallest flag vertically also achieves a slightly different look and sets it apart from the others.

OPPOSITE AND RIGHT: Glass display cases not only protect precious objects from exposure to dust, pets, and young children, but they can also be used as additional pieces of furniture in a room. This metal and glass case now acts as a bedside table. Designs like this one originally held merchandise on a store counter; today collectors search for them at flea markets and antiques malls.

good advice
Displaying one or two pieces of a collection separately from the rest makes the collection seem larger than it is.

MAKING OBJECTS LOOK THEIR BEST

OPPOSITE: When planning a ledge display that involves a number of different styles and materials, set up your foundations first, and then play with the placement of other objects until you find a look you love. The foundations on top of this built-in bookcase include the row of framed images leaning against the wall and the tall urn. Don't be afraid to mix fine works with children's art projects, antique prints, and family photographs. Using all of these pieces together will in fact create a more lively arrangement.

ABOVE: Pay attention to color and material when arranging objects that vary only slightly from one to another. These antique silhouettes and miniature portraits are all about the same size and shape, and yet their frames fall into two distinct groups: dark wood and gold. By alternating dark frames and gold frames, the colors are evenly distributed. Placing a single unrelated element at the end of the mantel adds visual interest. In place of the candlestick, a vase or figurine would work equally well.

BELOW: Positioned above a stove, plate racks can be both a decorative and a functional element in a kitchen. Not only will the plates, platters, and cups displayed in this manner look striking on the wall, they will also be at arm's reach when food needs to be transferred from stove to table. Racks can be left unpainted or coated any color that complements your room. Because this kitchen's woodwork is a soft green, the choice to paint the rack white makes it stand out even more. Concentrating the blue plates on the uppermost level draws the eye upward.

ABOVE: Glass-fronted cabinets protect prized possessions from dust. Cabinets with locking doors are good choices for preserving valuable antiques and heirlooms. An unexpected way to display seashells is by using them to stabilize flower stems at the bottom of a vase; a collection of beach stones or sea glass would also look lovely like this.

OPPOSITE: Shelves surrounding a kitchen window raise a collection of clear-glass cake stands, candy dishes, and pitchers from utilitarian to decorative status. Short shelves are perfectly proportioned to hold one cake stand apiece. Candy dishes and pitchers are each given their own shelf beneath the window. Simple shelves like these as well as the hardware needed to install them can be found at hardware and home-design stores.

MAKING OBJECTS LOOK THEIR BEST

OPPOSITE: To create the perfect spot for his antique potato mashers, one collector installed long, narrow shelves along a kitchen wall. The white background highlights design variations from one to the next. The gleaming black countertop underneath reflects the bottom row of mashers, making the collection appear even larger than it is.

RIGHT: In the evening, candlelight can be called on to cast a warm glow on collections. Such collections might be the candlesticks themselves, like the curvaceous brass designs on this mantel, or they might be silver platters, glass cake stands, or china teacups. Generally, anything with a shiny or reflective surface will look wonderful lighted in this manner.

MAKING OBJECTS LOOK THEIR BEST

LEFT AND ABOVE: In stark interiors, a single display unit is often all that is needed to showcase antiques and heirlooms. When in the market for a large piece, such as the cupboard in this elegant dining room, bring the dimensions of the space it will stand in, as well as the dimensions of the entryways to the room and the house. Arrangements that include more than one collection look great when the objects are organized by theme or material. Mercury glass occupies the left side of this cupboard; alabaster and pale green and blue wares are found on the opposite side.

OPPOSITE: When looking for furnishings that can be used for display, train your eye to spot potential in unexpected places. The backs of church pews are attached to the wall in this charming cottage. Painted white outside and black inside, they now act as racks for a collection of white iron-stone platters. The black interiors empha-size the graceful lines of the platters and harmonize with the entryway's accent color found in the armchair, the portions of wrought-iron fencing hung like artwork, and the inspirational words running along the top of the walls.

MAKING OBJECTS LOOK THEIR BEST

MAKING OBJECTS LOOK THEIR BEST

OPPOSITE AND ABOVE: Achieving the optimal setting for a collection may require building a special cabinet or installing lights to illuminate a dark wall in a hallway. For the owners of this house it meant decorating an entire room to match their collection of 1940s and '50s kitchenware. They set the stage with all-white walls and cabinetry and an old-fashioned black-and-white tile pattern on the floor. Next they chose reproduction vinyl-and-chrome chairs and stools; the red seats echo the bold hue of a set of tomato pottery. Finally, every nook and cranny was filled with mixing bowls, cookie jars, salt-and-pepper shakers, dish towels, and more. In fact, the countertops were so full that an additional small table had to be set near the window to accommodate the microwave.

OPPOSITE: A single shelf just below the ceiling is a great place to display collections. Not only does the high perch bestow added importance on the objects placed there, it is also well suited to homes with pets and small children. Shelves can run along one wall or around an entire room, like the example in this charming breakfast area. The yellowware and turquoise bowls echo the room's color scheme: Soft yellow hues characterize the woodwork and wallpaper, while light-blue paint unifies four vintage armchairs.

ABOVE: One creative home owner devised a fun way to showcase his collection of fish decoys in the bath. Attached to the wall with L-shaped hooks, the colorful pieces appear to swim. To achieve a seamless look, the hooks were painted the same deep green as the walls.

MAKING OBJECTS LOOK THEIR BEST

OPPOSITE: Curio shelves are ideal for drawing attention to each individual piece in a large collection. Shawnee miniatures are carefully arranged here. Such display units sometimes turn up at flea markets or thrift shops; a simple design like this one can also be duplicated by anyone with basic wood-shop skills or commissioned at a custom cabinetry store. The shelves can be painted the same shade as the walls or a slightly softer (or stronger) shade for contrast.

RIGHT: Positioning hanging shelves over a small table is an easy way to create an elegant display in any room in the house. In a dining room such as this one, china, glass, or silver are natural choices for display. Perfume bottles or figurines could enhance a bedroom or dressing area. Whatever you choose to arrange, leave enough breathing room between objects so that each can be viewed on its own. Playing with placement is also a good idea. Notice how in this shelving unit large pieces are placed on the top and bottom shelves, while more intricate groupings occupy the center.

MAKING OBJECTS LOOK THEIR BEST

four

Three of Anything Makes a Collection

YOU DON'T NEED TO SPEND A LIFETIME SCOURING ANTIQUES shops or break the bank to enjoy the benefits of decorating with collections. At *Country Living* we believe that it takes only three of any given object to constitute a collection. A trio of treasures creates a look that is simple and uncluttered. Groupings of this size are ideal for collectors who prefer pared-down interiors, for people who live in a small apartment or cottage, or for anyone who craves the flexibility of making (and rearranging) small displays out of larger collections. With such a small number of objects to work with, the approach to placement is greatly simplified. Rows work well for graduated sets or three items of the same size; a triangular arrangement of two pieces in the back and one in the front (or the other way around) makes up for mismatched heights. On these pages, we offer more than a dozen ideas for placing small collections around the house.

PRECEDING PAGES: In this pale-green bedroom, the contrast in size between the two collections on either side of the wardrobe and the large fashion photograph propped up behind them creates a playful look. To keep the arrangement from appearing overly symmetrical, a single green hobnail pitcher was placed on one side.

ABOVE: Setting objects at a slight angle gives figurines and figural items a sense of movement. These vintage jelly jars, for instance, look as if they might begin marching at any moment. Consider the dynamics of color when arranging collections; for instance, placing the red jar in the center of the trio creates a central point between the red spotted mixing bowl and the red Peter Pan bread box.

OPPOSITE: A trio of birdhouses suspended in front of a sunny window brings the joy of gardening indoors. Hanging the larger design on one side and the two smaller ones on the other balances the look while stimulating the eye. On the top shelf of the bookcase, a trio of decorative ceramic teapots repeats the three-of-a-kind theme.

Placing collections on related furnishings adds to the visual impact of an arrangement. A case in point is the row of small, medium, and large watering cans parading along a garden bench in this cottage living room. Other ideas might include setting teacups on a tea tray, candlesticks on a cake plate, or vintage sporting equipment on an old metal locker converted to storage in a mudroom.

THREE OF ANYTHING MAKES A COLLECTION

decorator's tip

Inspired by our nation's love affair with gardening, items originally intended for outdoor use are making their way indoors. A stately cast-iron urn can hold fresh flowers in the foyer, a well-worn wheelbarrow can store boots and umbrellas in the mud room, and terra-cotta flowerpots can organize pens and paperclips on a gardener's desk. Colorful sap buckets grace the wall in this dining room. Flea markets, salvage yards, and antique shows devoted to gardening tools and accessories are the best places to locate these objects.

OPPOSITE: The foyer is a perfect spot to introduce visitors to the collections you love. For this reason, small groupings work especially well in this setting. To balance the display on the small country table, a single large element—in this case, a weathered watering can—was placed opposite the row of polka-dotted pottery.

good advice

Graduated sets look wonderful when arranged in a row. Choose a prominent setting such as a windowsill or high shelf to attract maximum attention.

RIGHT: In an otherwise pared-down bath, three starfish add a touch of levity. What's more, they proclaim their owners' love of the sea. Other water-themed collections that would complement this setting while fitting snugly on this narrow ledge include seashells, river stones, beach glass, and vintage postcards of seaside destinations.

ABOVE: Collections need not be functional to make a statement. Vintage alarm clocks displaying various times of day rest on a bedside table. Clocks that no longer work can often be purchased for a song at flea markets. Look for designs that match the color scheme of a room; here, cream and chrome clocks complement the neutral setting.

OPPOSITE: The larger the display surface, the more room there is to play with placement. Although the clocks stand out as the main trio in this bedroom arrangement, other sets of three share the tabletop: three antique lace doilies supporting silver heirlooms, three glass vases, and three family photos gazing out from delicate frames.

THREE OF ANYTHING MAKES A COLLECTION

decorator's tip

Using mirrors to visually expand a small space has been a trick of the trade for quite a while. When thoughtfully placed beside a collection, mirrors can achieve the same effect. This stately mirror on a bedroom dresser not only brightens and expands the interior, it also instantly doubles the size of the collection displayed in front of it. The smaller mirror adds dimension and frames the bouquet. The dark wood mirror frames also add a touch of color to a room with white walls and white collections.

THREE OF ANYTHING MAKES A COLLECTION

good advice
Think creatively when arranging framed works of art; in addition to hanging them on the wall, consider leaning them against the wall behind a desk or laying them flat on a tabletop.

ABOVE: Three large mirrors make for a creative way of tackling a bare wall. The warm wooden tones of the frames reflect other furnishings found in the room, including the antique table and the bamboo armchair.

RIGHT: An antique farm table is an unusual place to find a row of frames, but many of the best ideas are found in unexpected places. Black-and-white photographs echo the checkerboard floor pattern in this hallway. Any small, framed pieces will work in a similar display: engravings, watercolors, or vintage postcards, just to name a few.

LEFT: Vintage milk bottles are just the vessels to hold large single blooms; in addition to sunflowers, other casual arrangements can be made with colorful African daisies or hydrangea stems. Some milk bottles found on the market-place bear enameled logos of dairies, while others are clear glass with embossed logos. You might either search for a color to match an interior or mix-and-match like this collector did.

OPPOSITE: Frequently found at flea markets and yard sales, similarly shaped bottles in varying sizes are ideal for floral arrange-ments because they can accommodate a range of blooms. Grouping them in a simple cluster enhances any tabletop. Clear bottles blend into neutral settings like this one; colored glass like ruby or emerald could be used to add a burst of color to the scene.

THREE OF ANYTHING MAKES A COLLECTION

OPPOSITE: Placement that is slightly askew is appropriate when the overall look of a room is more "shabby chic" than formal and elegant. In this vignette, the owners' love of weathered surfaces is evident: placing the three candlesticks in a loose triangle on one side of the table underscores the collectors' taste for imperfection.

RIGHT: A row of enamelware ewers fills a whitewashed dry sink. The large size of the pieces makes them well suited for the proportions of their setting. Subtle design variations in the enamelware enliven the all-white interior and help differentiate among the three similar objects. Ewers are immensely useful for holding fresh and dried flowers, evergreen branches, or fall foliage.

THREE OF ANYTHING MAKES A COLLECTION

photography credits

PAGE 1: Courtesy of *Country Living*

PAGE 2–3: Nick Bewsey and Nelson Zayas/
Gridley & Graves Photographers

PAGE 5 *(left to right)*: Keith Scott Morton;
Keith Scott Morton; Steven Mays;
Gridley & Graves

PAGE 6: Andrew McCaul

PAGE 8: Charles Maraia

PAGE 10: Jessie Walker

PAGE 11: John Gruen

PAGE 12: Michael Luppino

PAGE 13: Michael Skott

PAGE 14: Grey Crawford

PAGE 15: Steven Randazzo

PAGE 16: Michael Luppino

PAGE 17: Michael Luppino

PAGE 18–19: Michael Luppino

PAGE 21: Michael Luppino

PAGE 22: Keith Scott Morton

PAGE 23: Keith Scott Morton

PAGE 24: Courtesy of *Country Living*

PAGE 25: Keith Scott Morton

PAGE 26: Keith Scott Morton

PAGE 27: Keith Scott Morton

PAGE 28 *(top left)*: Keith Scott Morton

PAGE 28 *(bottom right)*: Keith Scott Morton

PAGE 29: Jeff McNamara

PAGE 30: Jeff McNamara

PAGE 31: Keith Scott Morton

PAGE 32: Jessie Walker

PAGE 33: Courtesy of *Country Living*

PAGE 34: Michael Luppino

PAGE 35: Paul Kopelow

PAGE 36 *(left)*: Dominique Vorillon

PAGE 36 *(right)*: David Prince

PAGE 37: Michael Luppino

PAGE 38: Keith Scott Morton

PAGE 39: Keith Scott Morton

PAGE 40: John Coolidge

PAGE 41: Michael Luppino

PAGE 42 *(left)*: Keith Scott Morton

PAGE 42 *(right)*: Keith Scott Morton

PAGE 43: David Prince

PAGE 44: Lisa Ishimuro/Gridley & Graves
Photographers

PAGE 45: Keith Scott Morton

PAGE 46: Steven Randazzo

PAGE 47: Steven Randazzo

PAGE 48: Keith Scott Morton

PAGE 49 *(left)*: Keith Scott Morton

PAGE 49 *(right)*: Steven Randazzo

PAGE 50: Julie Meris-Semel

PAGE 51: Keith Scott Morton

PAGE 52: Michael Luppino

PAGE 53: Steven Randazzo

PAGE 54: Keith Scott Morton

PAGE 55: Pizzo/Thompson Associates

PAGE 56: Steven Mark Needham

PAGE 57: David Prince

PAGE 58: Courtesy of *Country Living*

PAGE 59: Keith Scott Morton

PAGE 60 *(left)*: Keith Scott Morton

PAGE 60 *(right)*: Courtesy of *Country Living*

PAGE 61: Gridley & Graves Photographers

PAGE 62: Keith Scott Morton

PAGE 63: Grey Crawford

PAGE 64: John Bessler

PAGE 65: Keith Scott Morton

PAGE 66: Nick Bewsey & Nelson Zayas/
Gridley & Graves Photographers

PAGE 67: Michael Luppino

PAGE 68: Charles Maraia

PAGE 69: Keith Scott Morton

PAGE 70–71: Jeremy Samuelson

PAGE 73: Jessie Walker

PAGE 74: Paul Kopelow

PAGE 75: Keith Scott Morton

PAGE 76: Keith Scott Morton

PAGE 77: Keith Scott Morton

PAGE 78: Keith Scott Morton

PAGE 79: Keith Scott Morton

PAGE 80: Keith Scott Morton

PAGE 81: Courtesy of *Country Living*

PAGE 82: Keith Scott Morton

PAGE 83: Keith Scott Morton

PAGE 84: Michael Luppino

PAGE 85: Keith Scott Morton

PAGE 86: Keith Scott Morton

PAGE 87: Keith Scott Morton

PAGE 88: Keith Scott Morton

PAGE 89 *(left)*: Michael Luppino

PAGE 89 *(right)*: Keith Scott Morton

PAGE 90: Steven Randazzo

PAGE 91: Michael Luppino
PAGE 92: Steven Randazzo
PAGE 93: Michael Luppino
PAGE 94: Gridley & Graves Photographers
PAGE 95: Steven Randazzo
PAGE 96: Jeremy Samuelson
PAGE 97: Michael Luppino
PAGE 98 (left): Keith Scott Morton
PAGE 98 (right): Jessie Walker
PAGE 99: Keith Scott Morton
PAGE 100: John Bessler
PAGE 101: Steve Gross and Sue Daley
PAGE 102: Michael Luppino
PAGE 103: Steven Randazzo
PAGE 104: Michael Luppino
PAGE 105: Michael Luppino
PAGE 106: Jessie Walker
PAGE 107 (left): Keith Scott Morton
PAGE 107 (right): Keith Scott Morton
PAGE 108: Keith Scott Morton
PAGE 109: Keith Scott Morton
PAGE 110: Keith Scott Morton
PAGE 111: Keith Scott Morton
PAGE 112: Steven Randazzo
PAGE 113: Grey Crawford
PAGE 114: Keith Scott Morton
PAGE 115: Steven Randazzo
PAGE 116: Jessie Walker
PAGE 117: Keith Scott Morton
PAGE 118: Chuck Baker
PAGE 119: Courtesy of *Country Living*
PAGE 120: Keith Scott Morton
PAGE 121: Mark Lohman
PAGE 122–123: Grey Crawford
PAGE 125: Michael Luppino
PAGE 126: Keith Scott Morton
PAGE 127: Keith Scott Morton
PAGE 128: Keith Scott Morton
PAGE 129: Keith Scott Morton
PAGE 130: Keith Scott Morton

PAGE 131: Keith Scott Morton
PAGE 132: Keith Scott Morton
PAGE 133: Minh & Wass
PAGE 134: Michael Luppino
PAGE 135: Keith Scott Morton
PAGE 136: Courtesy of *Country Living*
PAGE 137: Courtesy of *Country Living*
PAGE 138: Minh & Wass
PAGE 139: Charles Maraia
PAGE 140: Jessie Walker
PAGE 141: Keith Scott Morton
PAGE 142: Keith Scott Morton
PAGE 143 (left): Keith Scott Morton
PAGE 143 (right): Keith Scott Morton
PAGE 144: Keith Scott Morton
PAGE 145: Steven Mays
PAGE 146: Keith Scott Morton
PAGE 147: Steven Randazzo
PAGE 148: Keith Scott Morton
PAGE 149 (top right): Jessie Walker
PAGE 149 (bottom left): Keith Scott Morton
PAGE 150: Steven Randazzo
PAGE 151: Keith Scott Morton
PAGE 152 (left): Keith Scott Morton
PAGE 152 (right): Keith Scott Morton
PAGE 153: Courtesy of *Country Living*
PAGE 154: Steve Gross & Sue Daley
PAGE 155: Steve Gross & Sue Daley
PAGE 156: David Prince
PAGE 157: Gridley & Graves
PAGE 158 (bottom left): Keith Scott Morton
PAGE 158 (top right): Michael Luppino
PAGE 159: Courtesy of *Country Living*
PAGE 160: Roger Cook
PAGE 161: Keith Scott Morton
PAGE 162 (left): Keith Scott Morton
PAGE 162 (right): Keith Scott Morton
PAGE 163: Keith Scott Morton
PAGE 164: Michael Luppino
PAGE 165: Michael Luppino

PAGE 166: Keith Scott Morton
PAGE 167: Julie Meris-Semel
PAGE 168: Keith Scott Morton
PAGE 169: Gridley & Graves Photographers
PAGE 170–171: Michael Luppino
PAGE 172: Courtesy of *Country Living*
PAGE 173: Gridley & Graves
PAGE 174: Keith Scott Morton
PAGE 175: Keith Scott Morton
PAGE 176: Keith Scott Morton
PAGE 177: William P. Steele
PAGE 178: Keith Scott Morton
PAGE 179: Keith Scott Morton
PAGE 180: Keith Scott Morton
PAGE 181 (left): Courtesy of *Country Living*
PAGE 181 (right): William P. Steele
PAGE 182: Gridley & Graves Photographers
PAGE 183: Charles Maraia
PAGE 184: Steven Randazzo
PAGE 185: John Coolidge

index